Object-Oriented
Programming in C++:

Creating Efficient, Maintainable, and Scalable Software
with Core OOP Principles, Design Strategies, and
Performance Optimization

Matthew D.Passmore

Table of Content

PART II: CORE OOP CONCEPTS IN C++

CHAPTER 3: Classes and Objects

Defining Classes and Objects
Constructors and Destructors
Access Modifiers: Public, Private, and Protected
Member Functions and Variables

CHAPTER 4: Encapsulation and Data Hiding

Implementing Data Encapsulation
Accessor and Mutator Functions
Getter and Setter Patterns

CHAPTER 5: Inheritance in C++

Base and Derived Classes

CHAPTER 1

Understanding Object-Oriented Programming (OOP)

Object-Oriented Programming (OOP) is a programming paradigm that organizes code around objects rather than functions. Objects combine data (attributes) and behavior (methods) to model real-world entities, making programs more intuitive and modular.

Key principles of OOP include:

Encapsulation: Combines data and methods within an object while restricting direct access to internal details. Abstraction: Focuses on essential features while hiding complexity.

Inheritance: Allows new classes to inherit properties and methods from existing ones, promoting code reuse. Polymorphism: Enables objects to take on multiple forms, simplifying code flexibility and extensibility. OOP enhances maintainability, scalability, and readability in software development.

What is OOP?

Object-Oriented Programming (OOP) is a programming paradigm that focuses on organizing code around "objects" rather than functions or procedures. These objects are instances of classes, which define the blueprint for the object's attributes (data) and methods (behavior). OOP is widely used in modern software development for its ability to model complex systems effectively.

Core Concepts of OOP:

Encapsulation: Combines data and behavior in a single unit while restricting unauthorized access, ensuring data integrity.

Abstraction: Hides complex implementation details and shows only the essential features to users.

Inheritance: Allows new classes to derive properties and methods from existing ones, enabling code reuse and hierarchical relationships.

Polymorphism: Permits objects and methods to take on multiple forms, making systems more flexible and extensible.

Benefits of OOP:

Modularity: Code can be divided into smaller, manageable pieces.
Reusability: Classes and objects can be reused across projects.
Scalability: Facilitates the development of large, complex applications.
Ease of Maintenance: Code is easier to debug, update, and extend.

OOP is a cornerstone of many programming languages, including C++, Java, Python, and C#. It is particularly effective for building software that reflects real-world systems, offering both clarity and efficiency in design.

The Evolution of OOP in C++

Object-Oriented Programming (OOP) in C++ has a rich history, evolving alongside the development of the language itself. C++ was designed to extend the capabilities of the C programming language by incorporating features that support OOP, enabling developers to write more modular, reusable, and maintainable code.

Key Milestones in the Evolution of OOP in C++:
The Birth of C++:

C++ was created by Bjarne Stroustrup in the early 1980s at Bell Labs.
Initially known as "C with Classes," it introduced classes and objects to C, paving the way for OOP.

Introduction of Core OOP Features:

Encapsulation: Classes allowed bundling of data and methods, with access specifiers like public, private, and protected.

Inheritance: Enabled hierarchical class structures, allowing code reuse across related classes.

Polymorphism: Introduced function overloading and virtual functions for dynamic method dispatch.

Standardization of C++:

The 1998 ISO C++ standard (C++98) established a formal specification for the language, solidifying its OOP foundations.

It included features like inheritance hierarchies, virtual destructors, and the Standard Template Library (STL) for generic programming.

Modern C++ (C++11 and Beyond):

C++11, C++14, and subsequent standards introduced features to enhance OOP:

Smart pointers (std::shared_ptr, std::unique_ptr) for memory management.

Move semantics for efficient object handling.

Lambda expressions, which complement functional programming within OOP.

These additions improved performance, safety, and clarity in OOP-based designs.

C++ Today:

Modern C++ continues to evolve, emphasizing performance and developer productivity.
The language integrates seamlessly with procedural, functional, and generic programming paradigms while retaining its strong support for OOP.

Impact of OOP in C++:

C++'s adoption of OOP transformed software engineering by enabling developers to model real-world systems with abstraction and reuse. Its influence is evident in a wide range of applications, from operating systems to games and embedded systems.

Core Principles of OOP: Encapsulation, Abstraction, Inheritance, and Polymorphism

Object-Oriented Programming (OOP) is built on four foundational principles that promote modularity, reusability, and clarity in software development. These principles are Encapsulation, Abstraction, Inheritance, and Polymorphism.

1. Encapsulation:

Encapsulation involves bundling data (attributes) and methods (functions) within a class while restricting direct access to the internal state. It ensures that an object's internal details are hidden from the outside world and can only be accessed or modified through controlled interfaces (getters and setters).

Benefits of Encapsulation:

Protects data integrity by preventing unauthorized access or modification.
Simplifies maintenance by isolating internal implementation details.
Promotes modularity and reusability.

Example in C++:

```cpp
Copy code
class Account {
private:
    double balance;
public:

    void deposit(double amount) { balance += amount; }
    double getBalance() const { return balance; }
};
```

2. Abstraction:

Abstraction focuses on hiding unnecessary details and exposing only the essential features of an object. It allows developers to work at a higher level of complexity without worrying about low-level implementation details.

Benefits of Abstraction:

Reduces complexity and enhances readability.

Promotes a clear separation of responsibilities.

Supports scalability by simplifying design.

Example in C++:

```cpp
Copy code
class Shape {
public:
    virtual void draw() const = 0; // Pure virtual function
};
class Circle : public Shape {
public:
    void draw() const override { cout << "Drawing Circle" << endl; }
};
```

3. Inheritance:

Inheritance allows a new class (derived class) to acquire properties and methods from an existing class (base class). It supports code reuse and establishes hierarchical relationships between classes.

Benefits of Inheritance:

Promotes code reuse, reducing redundancy.
Simplifies maintenance by centralizing shared behavior.
Enables the extension of existing functionality.
Example in C++:

```cpp
Copy code
class Animal {
public:
    void eat() { cout << "Eating" << endl; }
};
class Dog : public Animal {
public:
    void bark() { cout << "Barking" << endl; }
};
```

4. Polymorphism:

Polymorphism enables methods or objects to behave differently depending on the context. It comes in two forms:

Compile-time Polymorphism: Achieved through method overloading or operator overloading.
Runtime Polymorphism: Achieved through virtual functions and dynamic dispatch.

Benefits of Polymorphism:

Enhances flexibility and scalability.
Simplifies code by enabling a single interface for multiple implementations.
Reduces coupling by promoting interface-driven design.

Example in C++:

```cpp
Copy code
class Shape {
public:
```

```cpp
    virtual void draw() const { cout << "Drawing Shape"
<< endl; }
};
class Rectangle : public Shape {
public:
    void draw() const override { cout << "Drawing
Rectangle" << endl; }
};
```

These core principles work together to provide a solid foundation for building efficient, maintainable, and scalable object-oriented software.

CHAPTER 2

Setting Up the C++ Development Environment

To start programming in C++, you need to set up a suitable development environment. Here are the steps to get started:

1. Install a Compiler

A C++ compiler translates your code into executable programs. Popular options include:

GCC (GNU Compiler Collection): Available for Linux, macOS, and Windows (via MinGW or WSL).
MSVC (Microsoft Visual C++ Compiler): Bundled with Visual Studio for Windows.
Clang: Known for its performance and compatibility with modern C++ standards.

2. Choose an IDE or Text Editor

Integrated Development Environments (IDEs) simplify coding with features like syntax highlighting, debugging, and build tools. Popular choices include:

Visual Studio (Windows): Comprehensive IDE with MSVC integration.
CLion: A cross-platform IDE by JetBrains.
Code::Blocks or Dev-C++: Lightweight options for beginners.
Alternatively, use text editors like Visual Studio Code or Sublime Text with C++ extensions.

3. Set Up Build Tools

Ensure you have a build system to compile and link your programs:

Use Makefiles with GCC/Clang.
Employ CMake for cross-platform projects.

4. Write and Run a Simple Program
Open your IDE or editor.

Write a "Hello, World!" program:

cpp

Copy code

```cpp
#include <iostream>
using namespace std;

int main() {
    cout << "Hello, World!" << endl;
    return 0;
}
```

Compile and run the program using the IDE's build tools or a terminal command like:

bash

Copy code

```bash
g++ -o hello hello.cpp && ./hello
```

Setting up a robust environment ensures a smooth development experience and allows you to focus on mastering C++.

Installing Compilers and IDEs

To develop in C++, you need a compiler to translate code into executable programs and an Integrated Development Environment (IDE) or text editor to write, debug, and manage your code efficiently. Here's how to install popular compilers and IDEs:

1. Installing C++ Compilers

A compiler is essential for building C++ programs. Below are popular compiler options:

GCC (GNU Compiler Collection):

Available for Linux, macOS, and Windows (via MinGW or WSL).
Installation:
Linux: Install using the package manager, e.g., sudo apt install g++ (Ubuntu).
Windows: Use MinGW or MSYS2.
macOS: Install via Homebrew with brew install gcc.

MSVC (Microsoft Visual C++):

Comes with Microsoft Visual Studio, ideal for Windows development.

Installation:
Download Visual Studio from the Microsoft website.
Choose the "Desktop development with C++" workload during installation.

Clang:

Known for its speed and compatibility with modern C++ standards.

Installation:
Linux: Install via package manager, e.g., sudo apt install clang.
macOS: Included with Xcode or install via Homebrew (brew install llvm).
Windows: Install using LLVM or via WSL.

2. Installing IDEs

IDEs provide an integrated environment for coding, debugging, and building projects. Below are popular choices:

Visual Studio (Windows):

A comprehensive IDE with tools for debugging, profiling, and version control.

Installation:
Download the installer from Microsoft.
Choose the required workloads (e.g., "Desktop development with C++").

CLion (Cross-platform):

A powerful IDE by JetBrains with intelligent code analysis and CMake integration.

Installation:

Download from JetBrains.

Follow the setup instructions specific to your operating system.

Code::Blocks (Cross-platform):

A lightweight, beginner-friendly IDE.

Installation:

Download from Code::Blocks.

Install the version bundled with MinGW for Windows users.

Dev-C++ (Windows):

A simple IDE with a built-in compiler for C++ development.

Installation:

Download from the Dev-C++ website.

Visual Studio Code (Cross-platform):

A lightweight editor with C++ extensions for debugging and IntelliSense.

Installation:
Download from VS Code.
Install the C++ extension pack.

3. Testing Your Setup
Once installed:

Write a "Hello, World!" program in your IDE or editor.
Compile and run it using the IDE's build tools or terminal commands.
Ensure the compiler and IDE are properly integrated for a seamless development experience.

Having the right tools simplifies the process of writing, debugging, and optimizing C++ code.

Writing Your First C++ Program

Writing your first C++ program is a simple and exciting step in learning the language. A common starting point is creating a "Hello, World!" program that displays a message on the screen. Here's how you can write, compile, and run your first program:

1. Setting Up Your Environment
Ensure you have:

A C++ compiler installed (e.g., GCC, MSVC, or Clang).
An IDE or text editor (e.g., Visual Studio, CLion, Code::Blocks, or VS Code).

2. Writing the Program

Open your IDE or text editor.
Create a new file and name it hello.cpp (C++ source files typically have the .cpp extension).

Write the following code:

cpp

Copy code

```cpp
#include <iostream> // Include the input-output stream library
using namespace std; // Use the standard namespace

int main() {
    cout << "Hello, World!" << endl; // Print "Hello, World!" to the console
    return 0; // Indicate that the program executed successfully
}
```

3. Compiling the Program

To convert your code into an executable file:

Using a terminal or command prompt:
Navigate to the folder containing hello.cpp.
Run the compiler command:
GCC: g++ hello.cpp -o hello
Clang: clang++ hello.cpp -o hello

This generates an executable file named hello (or hello.exe on Windows).

Using an IDE:
Use the IDE's "Build" or "Compile" feature to create the executable.

4. Running the Program

In a terminal:
Execute the program:
On Linux/macOS: ./hello
On Windows: hello

In an IDE:

Use the "Run" button to execute the program.
The output should display:

Copy code
Hello, World!

5. Understanding the Code

#include <iostream>: Includes the library needed for input and output.

using namespace std;: Simplifies access to standard library functions.

int main(): Defines the program's entry point.

cout << "Hello, World!": Outputs the message to the console.

return 0;: Signals the program executed successfully.

Congratulations! You've written and executed your first C++ program, a foundational step toward mastering the language.

Introduction to C++ Syntax and Structure

C++ is a statically typed, compiled programming language that follows a structured and organized syntax.

Its syntax is based on C, but it introduces features for object-oriented, procedural, and generic programming. Understanding the basic syntax and structure of a C++ program is essential for writing efficient code.

1. General Structure of a C++ Program

A simple C++ program consists of the following key components:

cpp
Copy code

```cpp
#include <iostream>  // Preprocessor directive
using namespace std; // Namespace declaration

int main() {      // Main function
    cout << "Hello, World!" << endl; // Output statement
    return 0;     // Return statement
}
```

2. Key Elements of C++ Syntax

Preprocessor Directives:

Lines beginning with # are preprocessor directives.
Example: #include <iostream> includes the input/output
library.

Namespaces:

using namespace std; allows access to the standard
library without prefixing std::.

Main Function:

The entry point of a C++ program is the main() function.
Syntax: int main() { /* code */ return 0; }.
Statements:

End with a semicolon (;).
Example: cout << "Hello, World!";.
Comments:

Single-line: // This is a comment.
Multi-line: /* This is a comment */.

3. Basic Syntax Rules

Case Sensitivity: C++ is case-sensitive (Main is different from main).

White Space: Ignored by the compiler but used for code readability.

Blocks and Scope:

Curly braces {} define blocks of code.

Variables and functions declared within blocks have limited scope.

4. Common Language Constructs

Variables and Data Types:

Declared with a type, name, and optionally, an initial value.

Example:

cpp
Copy code

```cpp
int age = 25;
float pi = 3.14;
```

Control Statements:

if, else, switch for decision-making.
for, while, do-while for loops.

Functions:

Reusable blocks of code.
Syntax:
cpp
Copy code
```cpp
int add(int a, int b) {
    return a + b;
}
```

Input/Output:

cin for input and cout for output.
Example:
cpp

Copy code

```
int x;
cin >> x; // Takes input from the user
cout << "You entered: " << x << endl;
```

Object-Oriented Features:

C++ supports classes and objects for OOP.

Example:

cpp

Copy code

```
class Car {
public:
    void drive() { cout << "Driving" << endl; }
};
```

5. Best Practices

Use meaningful variable names for clarity.

Follow consistent indentation and formatting.

Comment code to explain logic and increase maintainability.

By mastering C++ syntax and structure, you lay the foundation for writing robust and efficient programs.

PART II: CORE OOP CONCEPTS IN C++

CHAPTER 3
Classes and Objects

Classes and objects are fundamental concepts in C++'s object-oriented programming paradigm. They provide a blueprint for organizing and managing data and behavior in a structured way.

1. Classes

A class is a user-defined data type that serves as a blueprint for creating objects. It defines the properties (data members) and behaviors (member functions) of the objects.

Example:

cpp
Copy code
```cpp
class Car {
```

```cpp
public:          // Access specifier
    string brand;   // Data member
    int speed;      // Data member

    void drive() {  // Member function
        cout << "The car is driving at " << speed << " km/h." << endl;
    }
};
```

2. Objects

An object is an instance of a class. It represents a specific entity that can hold data and use the behaviors defined by its class.

Example:

cpp
Copy code
```cpp
int main() {
    Car myCar;          // Create an object
    myCar.brand = "Toyota"; // Set data members
```

```
    myCar.speed = 120;

    myCar.drive();        // Call member function
    return 0;
}
```

Output:

bash
Copy code
The car is driving at 120 km/h.

Key Features

Encapsulation: Groups related data and functions together.
Abstraction: Hides unnecessary details and exposes only essential features.
Reuse: Classes can be reused to create multiple objects with shared behavior.
Using classes and objects in C++ promotes code modularity, scalability, and maintainability.

Defining Classes and Objects

In C++, classes and objects are the building blocks of object-oriented programming. A class defines a blueprint for creating objects, encapsulating data (attributes) and behaviors (methods). An object is an instance of a class, representing a concrete implementation of its blueprint.

1. Defining a Class

A class in C++ is defined using the class keyword, followed by the class name and a pair of curly braces containing its members. Members include:

Attributes: Variables that hold the data of the class.
Methods: Functions that define the behavior of the class.

Syntax:

```cpp
Copy code
class ClassName {
public:          // Access specifier
   // Attributes (data members)
   // Methods (member functions)
};
```

Example:

```cpp
Copy code
class Car {
public:
   string brand;   // Attribute
   int speed;      // Attribute

   void drive() { // Method
     cout << "Driving at " << speed << " km/h." << endl;
   }
```

};

2. Creating Objects

An object is created by declaring a variable of the class type. Once created, objects can access the class's public members using the dot operator (.).

Example:

cpp
Copy code
```cpp
int main() {
    Car myCar;              // Create an object
    myCar.brand = "Tesla";  // Set attributes
    myCar.speed = 100;

    myCar.drive();          // Call method
    return 0;
}
```
Output:

bash

Copy code
Driving at 100 km/h.

3. Access Specifiers

Classes in C++ use access specifiers to control the visibility of their members:

public: Members are accessible from outside the class.
private: Members are accessible only within the class.
protected: Members are accessible within the class and derived classes.
Example:

cpp
Copy code
```
class Person {
private:
    string name;

public:
    void setName(string n) { name = n; }
    string getName() { return name; }
```

```
};
```

4. Key Points

Classes promote encapsulation, grouping data and functions together.

Objects allow modularity, enabling reuse of code with different states.

Using access specifiers ensures data security and abstraction.

By defining classes and objects effectively, C++ programs become more structured, maintainable, and scalable.

Constructors and Destructors

Constructors and destructors are special member functions in C++ that play a crucial role in object lifecycle management. They initialize and clean up resources for objects.

1. Constructors

A constructor is a special member function that is automatically called when an object of a class is created. It is used to initialize the object's attributes or allocate resources.

Key Characteristics:

The constructor has the same name as the class.
It has no return type (not even void).
It can be overloaded to accept different sets of parameters.

Types of Constructors:

Default Constructor:

Takes no arguments and initializes attributes with default values.

cpp

```
Copy code
class Car {
public:
    string brand;
    int speed;

    Car() { // Default constructor
        brand = "Unknown";
        speed = 0;
    }
};
```

Parameterized Constructor:

Takes arguments to initialize attributes with specific values.

```cpp
Copy code
class Car {
public:
    string brand;
    int speed;
```

```cpp
    Car(string b, int s) { // Parameterized constructor
        brand = b;
        speed = s;
    }
};
```

Copy Constructor:

Initializes an object by copying another object of the same class.

cpp
Copy code
```cpp
class Car {
public:
    string brand;

    Car(const Car &obj) { // Copy constructor
        brand = obj.brand;
    }
};
```

Example:

cpp

Copy code

```cpp
int main() {
    Car car1("Tesla", 120);  // Parameterized constructor
    cout << car1.brand << " is driving at " << car1.speed << " km/h." << endl;
    return 0;
}
```

2. Destructors

A destructor is a special member function that is automatically called when an object goes out of scope or is explicitly deleted. It is used to release resources, such as memory or file handles.

Key Characteristics:

The destructor has the same name as the class, preceded by a tilde (~).
It has no parameters and no return type.
Each class has only one destructor (cannot be overloaded).

Example:

```cpp
Copy code
class Car {
public:
    Car() {
        cout << "Constructor: Object created." << endl;
    }

    ~Car() {
        cout << "Destructor: Object destroyed." << endl;
    }
};

int main() {
    Car myCar; // Constructor is called
    return 0; // Destructor is called automatically
}
```

Output:

vbnet

Copy code

Constructor: Object created.

Destructor: Object destroyed.

3. Usage in Resource Management

Constructors initialize attributes and allocate resources like dynamic memory or file handles.
Destructors clean up resources to avoid memory leaks or dangling pointers.
Example with Dynamic Memory:

cpp
Copy code

```cpp
class Array {
private:
    int* data;
    int size;

public:
    Array(int n) { // Constructor
        size = n;
        data = new int[size];
```

```cpp
    cout << "Array created with size " << size << "." <<
endl;
  }

  ~Array() { // Destructor
    delete[] data;
    cout << "Array destroyed." << endl;
  }
};
```

4. Key Points

Always define a destructor when using dynamic memory
or resources.
Use constructors to simplify object initialization.
Constructors and destructors improve code readability
and manage resource lifecycles efficiently.

Access Modifiers: Public, Private, and Protected

Access modifiers in C++ are used to control the visibility and accessibility of class members (attributes and methods). They play a crucial role in implementing data encapsulation, a core principle of object-oriented programming (OOP). C++ provides three primary access modifiers: public, private, and protected.

1. Public Access Modifier

The public keyword allows members to be accessed from anywhere in the program. This means both other classes and external functions can interact with public members directly. It is commonly used for functions and attributes that need to be accessible from outside the class.

Key Characteristics:

Members are accessible from within the class, derived classes, and outside the class.
Typically used for methods that form the class's interface.

Example:

```cpp
Copy code
class Car {
public:
    string brand; // Public attribute

    void displayBrand() { // Public method
        cout << "Car brand: " << brand << endl;
    }
};

int main() {
    Car myCar;
    myCar.brand = "Toyota"; // Direct access to public attribute
    myCar.displayBrand();   // Direct access to public method
    return 0;
}
```

Output:

```yaml
Copy code
Car brand: Toyota
```

2. Private Access Modifier

The private keyword restricts access to members only within the class where they are declared. These members cannot be accessed directly by derived classes or external code. Private access is typically used for attributes that need protection from direct modification.

Key Characteristics:

Members are accessible only within the defining class.
Used to encapsulate and protect sensitive data.

Example:

```cpp
Copy code
class BankAccount {
private:
    double balance;  // Private attribute
```

```cpp
public:
    void setBalance(double amount) { // Public method
to modify balance
        if (amount >= 0) {
            balance = amount;
        } else {
            cout << "Invalid balance amount!" << endl;
        }
    }

    double getBalance() {   // Public method to access
balance
        return balance;
    }
};

int main() {
    BankAccount myAccount;
    myAccount.setBalance(500.0);    // Accessing private
attribute via public method
    cout << "Balance: $" << myAccount.getBalance() <<
endl; // Accessing balance
```

```cpp
    return 0;
}
```
Output:

bash
Copy code
Balance: $500

3. Protected Access Modifier

The protected keyword is similar to private, but with one key difference: protected members are accessible in derived classes. This modifier is useful when you want to allow derived classes to access certain members while keeping them hidden from external code.

Key Characteristics:
Members are accessible within the defining class and derived classes.
Commonly used in inheritance scenarios.

Example:
cpp

```cpp
Copy code
class Parent {
protected:
    int protectedValue;  // Protected attribute

public:
    void setProtectedValue(int value) {
        protectedValue = value;
    }
};

class Child : public Parent {
public:
    void displayValue() {
        cout << "Protected Value: " << protectedValue <<
endl;  // Accessing inherited protected member
    }
};

int main() {
    Child obj;
    obj.setProtectedValue(42);  // Setting value using
parent method
```

```
    obj.displayValue();          // Accessing protected
member in derived class
    return 0;
}
```

Output:

mathematica

Copy code

Protected Value: 42

Comparison Table

Modifier	Access Within Class	Access in Derived Class	Access Outside Class
Public	Yes	Yes	Yes
Private	Yes	No	No
Protected	Yes	Yes	No

Practical Use Cases

Public: For methods or attributes that define the class interface (e.g., display() functions).

Private: For sensitive data that should not be accessed or modified directly (e.g., account balance, passwords).

Protected: For attributes or methods intended for use only in inheritance hierarchies (e.g., shared functionality between base and derived classes).

By effectively using access modifiers, C++ developers can control data access, maintain encapsulation, and create secure, maintainable, and well-structured programs.

Member Functions and Variables

In C++, member functions and member variables are the foundational components of a class. They enable classes to encapsulate data (variables) and behavior (functions), adhering to object-oriented programming principles.

1. Member Variables

Member variables, also known as data members, are attributes defined within a class to hold the state or properties of an object. They are typically declared in the class definition and can have different access specifiers: public, private, or protected.

Characteristics:

Each object of the class has its own copy of member variables unless declared static.
Their scope is limited to the class they belong to.

Example:
cpp
Copy code

```cpp
class Car {
public:
    string brand;  // Public member variable
    int speed;     // Public member variable
```

private:

   double price; // Private member variable
};

2. Member Functions

Member functions, also called methods, are functions defined within a class that operate on the class's data members. They can perform actions, modify the state of an object, or provide access to private/protected members.

Characteristics:

Can access and modify both member variables and other member functions.
Defined either inside the class definition (inline) or outside it (using the scope resolution operator ::).
Can have different access specifiers.

Example:

cpp

```
Copy code
class Car {
public:
    string brand;
    int speed;

    // Member function
    void displayDetails() {
        cout << "Brand: " << brand << ", Speed: " << speed << " km/h" << endl;
    }
};
```

Types of Member Functions

Accessor Functions: Used to access private/protected variables (e.g., getters).

Mutator Functions: Used to modify private/protected variables (e.g., setters).

Constructor: Special member function for initializing objects.

Destructor: Special member function for cleaning up resources.

Static Functions: Operate at the class level and are not tied to any specific object.

3. Defining Member Functions Outside the Class

Member functions can be defined outside the class using the scope resolution operator (::). This separates the function's declaration in the class and its implementation elsewhere in the code.

Example:
cpp
Copy code
```cpp
class Rectangle {
private:
    int width, height;

public:
    // Declaration
    void setDimensions(int w, int h);
    int calculateArea();
};
```

```
// Definition outside the class
void Rectangle::setDimensions(int w, int h) {
    width = w;
    height = h;
}

int Rectangle::calculateArea() {
    return width * height;
}

int main() {
    Rectangle rect;
    rect.setDimensions(5, 10);
    cout << "Area: " << rect.calculateArea() << endl;
    return 0;
}
```

Output:

makefile
Copy code
Area: 50

4. Static Members

Static members (variables and functions) belong to the class rather than any specific object. They are shared among all objects of the class.

Example:

cpp
Copy code

```cpp
class Counter {
private:
    static int count; // Static member variable

public:
    Counter() {
        count++;
    }

    static int getCount() { // Static member function
        return count;
    }
};
```

```
// Initialize static variable
int Counter::count = 0;
```

```cpp
int main() {
    Counter c1, c2, c3;
    cout << "Total objects: " << Counter::getCount() <<
endl;
    return 0;
}
```
Output:

mathematica
Copy code
Total objects: 3

Summary

Member Variables: Hold data relevant to the object; can be public, private, or protected.
Member Functions: Define the behavior of the class and manipulate its data.

Together, they enable a class to encapsulate state and behavior, providing a blueprint for creating objects in C++.

CHAPTER 4

Encapsulation and Data Hiding

Encapsulation and data hiding are fundamental concepts in object-oriented programming, ensuring data security and promoting modular code design.

Encapsulation

Encapsulation is the process of bundling data (variables) and methods (functions) that operate on the data into a single unit, i.e., a class. It restricts direct access to certain components and provides controlled access through methods.

Key Features:

Groups related data and functions together.
Promotes code modularity and maintainability.
Simplifies debugging by isolating functionality.

Example:

```cpp
Copy code
class Car {
private:
    int speed; // Encapsulated data

public:
    void setSpeed(int s) { speed = s; } // Controlled access
    int getSpeed() { return speed; }
};
```

Data Hiding

Data hiding restricts direct access to class attributes, protecting them from unintended modifications. This is achieved by declaring attributes as private or protected and providing public getter and setter methods for controlled access.

Benefits:

Prevents unauthorized access and ensures data integrity. Encourages abstraction by hiding implementation details.

Example:

cpp
Copy code
```cpp
class BankAccount {
private:
    double balance;  // Hidden data

public:
    void deposit(double amount) { balance += amount; }
    double getBalance() { return balance; }
};
```

Encapsulation and data hiding enhance security, abstraction, and reusability, making programs more robust and maintainable.

Implementing Data Encapsulation

Data encapsulation is the practice of bundling data and methods into a single unit, typically a class, and restricting direct access to the data to ensure its security and integrity. This is achieved by declaring attributes as private or protected and providing public methods to access or modify them.

Steps to Implement Data Encapsulation
Declare Attributes as Private or Protected

Restrict direct access to the data by using private or protected access specifiers.
Provide Public Getter and Setter Methods

Use public member functions to provide controlled access to the data.

Getters retrieve the value of private attributes, while setters modify them.

Enforce Validation in Setter Methods

Implement validation logic in setters to prevent invalid or unsafe operations.

Example:

cpp
Copy code

```cpp
#include <iostream>
using namespace std;

class Employee {
private:
    int id;          // Encapsulated attribute
    string name;     // Encapsulated attribute
    double salary;   // Encapsulated attribute

public:
    // Setter for ID
    void setId(int employeeId) {
        if (employeeId > 0) {  // Validation
            id = employeeId;
        } else {
            cout << "Invalid ID!" << endl;
```

```
    }
  }

  // Getter for ID
  int getId() {
    return id;
  }

  // Setter for Name
  void setName(string employeeName) {
    name = employeeName;
  }

  // Getter for Name
  string getName() {
    return name;
  }

  // Setter for Salary
  void setSalary(double employeeSalary) {
    if (employeeSalary >= 0) { // Validation
      salary = employeeSalary;
    } else {
```

```cpp
            cout << "Invalid Salary!" << endl;
        }
    }

    // Getter for Salary
    double getSalary() {
        return salary;
    }
};

int main() {
    Employee emp;

    // Setting attributes using setter methods
    emp.setId(101);
    emp.setName("John Doe");
    emp.setSalary(50000);

    // Accessing attributes using getter methods
    cout << "Employee ID: " << emp.getId() << endl;
    cout << "Employee Name: " << emp.getName() << endl;
```

```cpp
    cout << "Employee Salary: $" << emp.getSalary() <<
endl;

    return 0;
}
```
Output:
yaml
Copy code
Employee ID: 101
Employee Name: John Doe
Employee Salary: $50000

Advantages of Data Encapsulation

Data Security: Prevents unauthorized or accidental modifications.

Abstraction: Hides implementation details and exposes only necessary information.

Maintainability: Simplifies debugging and future updates.

Flexibility: Allows validation and controlled updates through setter methods.

By implementing data encapsulation, C++ programs become more secure, robust, and easier to maintain.

Accessor and Mutator Functions

In object-oriented programming, accessor and mutator functions are commonly used to provide controlled access to an object's private attributes. They are essential for maintaining data encapsulation, ensuring that the internal state of an object is protected and can only be modified or accessed through well-defined interfaces.

1. Accessor Functions (Getters)

An accessor function (also known as a getter) is a method that retrieves the value of a private attribute. It does not modify the state of the object, and it only provides read access to the data.

Key Characteristics:

It returns the value of a private member variable.

It typically has no side effects and does not alter the state of the object.

It is declared as a public method to allow external code to access private data.

Example:

cpp

Copy code

```
class Employee {
private:
    string name; // Private attribute

public:
    // Accessor function
    string getName() {
        return name;
    }
};
```

Usage:

```cpp
Copy code
Employee emp;
cout << emp.getName(); // Accessing the name via the
accessor function
```

2. Mutator Functions (Setters)

A mutator function (also known as a setter) is a method that modifies the value of a private attribute. It allows controlled modification of the object's internal state and can include validation to ensure that only valid data is set.

Key Characteristics:

It changes the value of a private member variable.
It may include validation or other logic to maintain data integrity.
It is declared as a public method to allow external code to modify the data.

Example:

cpp

Copy code

```cpp
class Employee {
private:
    int salary; // Private attribute

public:
    // Mutator function
    void setSalary(int s) {
        if (s > 0) {
            salary = s; // Valid salary
        } else {
            cout << "Salary must be positive!" << endl;
        }
    }
};
```

Usage:

cpp

Copy code

```cpp
Employee emp;
```

emp.setSalary(50000); // Modifying the salary via the mutator function

---

Example of Both Accessor and Mutator Functions Together

Here's an example of a class using both accessor and mutator functions to manage private data:

cpp
Copy code

```cpp
#include <iostream>
using namespace std;

class Car {
private:
    string brand;  // Private attribute
    int year;      // Private attribute

public:
    // Mutator function (Setter)
    void setBrand(string b) {
        brand = b;
```

```cpp
    }

    // Accessor function (Getter)
    string getBrand() {
        return brand;
    }

    // Mutator function (Setter)
    void setYear(int y) {
        if (y > 0) {
            year = y;
        } else {
            cout << "Invalid year!" << endl;
        }
    }

    // Accessor function (Getter)
    int getYear() {
        return year;
    }
};

int main() {
```

```cpp
    Car myCar;
    myCar.setBrand("Toyota");    // Setting the brand using mutator
    myCar.setYear(2020);         // Setting the year using mutator

    cout << "Car Brand: " << myCar.getBrand() << endl;  // Getting the brand using accessor
    cout << "Car Year: " << myCar.getYear() << endl;   // Getting the year using accessor

    return 0;
}
```

Output:

yaml
Copy code
Car Brand: Toyota
Car Year: 2020

Advantages of Accessor and Mutator Functions

Encapsulation: They maintain the principle of data encapsulation by hiding the internal state of an object and providing controlled access.

Data Integrity: Mutators can enforce validation and prevent invalid data from being set, ensuring the object remains in a valid state.

Flexibility: Accessor and mutator functions allow easy modification of internal implementation without changing the external interface of the class.

Maintainability: They make code easier to maintain and debug, as changes to the class internals can be isolated to these functions.

By using accessor and mutator functions, C++ developers can create more robust, maintainable, and secure code, ensuring that object states are only manipulated in intended ways.

Getter and Setter Patterns

The getter and setter patterns are fundamental techniques in object-oriented programming used to access and modify an object's private data. These patterns enforce data encapsulation, allowing controlled interaction with an object's internal state while maintaining the integrity of the data. They are implemented through accessor (getter) and mutator (setter) methods.

1. Getter Pattern (Accessor)

A getter method, also known as an accessor, is used to retrieve the value of a private attribute. The getter provides read-only access to the data, ensuring that it cannot be modified directly from outside the class. This pattern promotes data encapsulation, allowing the class to protect its internal state.

Characteristics of a Getter:

Retrieves the value of a private member variable.
Returns the value without modifying the object's state.
Provides controlled access to an object's attributes.

Example:

cpp
Copy code

```cpp
class Rectangle {
private:
    int width;  // Private member variable
    int height; // Private member variable

public:
    // Getter for width
    int getWidth() const {
        return width;
    }

    // Getter for height
    int getHeight() const {
        return height;
    }
};
```

2. Setter Pattern (Mutator)

A setter method, also known as a mutator, is used to set or modify the value of a private attribute. The setter provides write access to the internal state of the object, allowing controlled updates. It is common to include validation logic inside the setter to ensure that only valid data is assigned.

Characteristics of a Setter:

Modifies the value of a private member variable.
Can include validation or other logic to ensure data integrity.

Provides controlled write access to the object's attributes.

Example:
cpp
Copy code
class Rectangle {
private:
   int width; // **Private member variable**
   int height; // **Private member variable**

```cpp
public:
    // Setter for width
    void setWidth(int w) {
        if (w > 0) {
            width = w;
        } else {
            cout << "Width must be greater than 0!" << endl;
        }
    }


    // Setter for height
    void setHeight(int h) {
        if (h > 0) {
            height = h;
        } else {
            cout << "Height must be greater than 0!" << endl;
        }
    }
};
```

Example: Full Implementation of Getter and Setter Patterns

```cpp
Copy code
#include <iostream>
using namespace std;

class Circle {
private:
    double radius; // Private attribute

public:
    // Getter for radius
    double getRadius() const {
        return radius;
    }

    // Setter for radius with validation
    void setRadius(double r) {
        if (r > 0) {
            radius = r;
        } else {
```

```cpp
            cout << "Radius must be positive!" << endl;
        }
    }

    // Function to calculate the area
    double calculateArea() const {
        return 3.14159 * radius * radius;
    }
};

int main() {
    Circle myCircle;

    // Using setter to set radius
    myCircle.setRadius(5.0);

    // Using getter to get radius
    cout << "Circle radius: " << myCircle.getRadius() << endl;

    // Using method to calculate area
    cout << "Circle area: " << myCircle.calculateArea() << endl;
```

```
    return 0;
}
```

Output:

mathematica
Copy code
Circle radius: 5
Circle area: 78.5398

Advantages of Getter and Setter Patterns

Data Integrity: Setters can enforce rules and validation to ensure that only valid data is set, preventing invalid states in the object.

Flexibility: These methods allow the class implementation to change without affecting external code that interacts with the class.

Encapsulation: Getters and setters hide the internal workings of the object, exposing only necessary methods to interact with the object, keeping the internal state secure.

Control: By controlling how data is accessed and modified, these patterns make it easier to maintain, update, or extend the class in the future.

Debugging and Logging: Getters and setters can easily be modified to include additional functionality, such as logging, tracking changes, or adding debugging features.

When to Use Getter and Setter Patterns

Encapsulation: Use getters and setters when you need to encapsulate your data and control how it is accessed and modified.

Data Validation: When you want to ensure that data passed to an object meets specific conditions (e.g., positive values, valid ranges).

Read-Only or Write-Only Data: You can use getters for read-only data and setters for write-only data.

Maintainability: These patterns make it easier to maintain and modify classes, especially as they evolve over time.

By using getter and setter patterns, C++ programs can achieve cleaner, more modular, and maintainable code.

This design approach ensures that the internal state of objects is protected and that interactions with objects are controlled and predictable.

Inheritance is a core concept in object-oriented programming (OOP) that allows a class (called the derived class) to inherit attributes and behaviors (member variables and functions) from another class (called the base class). This promotes code reuse and helps in building hierarchical class structures.

Key Features of Inheritance:

Code Reusability: Common functionality can be defined in a base class and reused in derived classes.

Extensibility: New features can be added to derived classes without modifying the base class.

Hierarchy: Allows the creation of a class hierarchy, enabling modular and organized code.

Syntax of Inheritance:

cpp

Copy code

```
class BaseClass {
    // Members of the base class
};


class DerivedClass : public BaseClass {
    // Members of the derived class
};
```

Types of Inheritance in C++:

Single Inheritance: A class inherits from one base class.

Multiple Inheritance: A class inherits from more than one base class.

Multilevel Inheritance: A class inherits from a derived class, forming a chain.

Hierarchical Inheritance: Multiple classes inherit from the same base class.

Hybrid Inheritance: A combination of two or more types of inheritance.

Example:

Single Inheritance:

```cpp
#include <iostream>
using namespace std;

class Animal {
public:
   void eat() {
      cout << "This animal eats food." << endl;
   }
};

class Dog : public Animal {
public:
   void bark() {
      cout << "The dog barks." << endl;
   }
};

int main() {
   Dog myDog;
   myDog.eat(); // Inherited from Animal
```

```
    myDog.bark(); // Defined in Dog
    return 0;
}
```

Output:

Copy code
This animal eats food.
The dog barks.

Access Specifiers and Inheritance:

Public Inheritance: Public and protected members of the base class remain public and protected in the derived class.

Protected Inheritance: Public and protected members of the base class become protected in the derived class.

Private Inheritance: Public and protected members of the base class become private in the derived class.

Inheritance simplifies the creation of modular, reusable, and maintainable code structures, enabling efficient software development.

Base and Derived Classes

In C++, base classes and derived classes form the backbone of inheritance, a key feature of object-oriented programming (OOP). A base class (or parent class) provides common functionality that can be inherited and extended by a derived class (or child class).

Base Classes

A base class serves as the blueprint from which other classes (derived classes) inherit. It contains attributes (member variables) and methods (member functions) that can be reused or overridden by derived classes.

Key Points:

Defines common behavior for multiple derived classes. Can include members with different access specifiers: public, private, or protected.

Example:

cpp

Copy code

```cpp
class Vehicle {
public:
  void start() {
    cout << "Vehicle started" << endl;
  }
};
```

Derived Classes

A derived class inherits attributes and behaviors from a base class. It can also add its own unique attributes and methods or override the base class methods.

Key Points:

Inherits members from the base class according to the specified access mode (public, protected, private).
Can extend or modify the base class functionality.

Example:

cpp

Copy code

```cpp
class Car : public Vehicle {  // 'Car' is a derived class
public:
  void drive() {
    cout << "Car is driving" << endl;
  }
};
```

Base and Derived Class Relationship

Syntax:

cpp

Copy code

```cpp
class BaseClass {
  // Base class members
};

class DerivedClass : access_mode BaseClass {
  // Derived class members
};
```

Example:

cpp

```
Copy code
#include <iostream>
using namespace std;

class Animal { // Base class
public:
  void eat() {
    cout << "This animal eats food." << endl;
  }
};

class Dog : public Animal { // Derived class
public:
  void bark() {
    cout << "The dog barks." << endl;
  }
};

int main() {
  Dog myDog;
  myDog.eat();  // Accessing base class method
  myDog.bark(); // Accessing derived class method
  return 0;
```

}
Output:

Copy code
This animal eats food.
The dog barks.

Access Control in Base and Derived Classes

Public Inheritance: Public and protected members of the base class retain their access levels in the derived class.
Protected Inheritance: Public and protected members of the base class become protected in the derived class.
Private Inheritance: Public and protected members of the base class become private in the derived class.

Base Class and Constructor/Destructor in Derived Classes

Constructors: The base class constructor is invoked automatically before the derived class constructor.
Destructors: The derived class destructor is executed first, followed by the base class destructor.

Example:

cpp

Copy code

```cpp
class Base {
public:
  Base() {
    cout << "Base class constructor" << endl;
  }
  ~Base() {
    cout << "Base class destructor" << endl;
  }
};

class Derived : public Base {
public:
  Derived() {
    cout << "Derived class constructor" << endl;
  }
  ~Derived() {
    cout << "Derived class destructor" << endl;
  }
};
```

```
int main() {
    Derived obj;
    return 0;
}
```
Output:

kotlin

Copy code

Base class constructor

Derived class constructor

Derived class destructor

Base class destructor

Advantages of Base and Derived Classes

Code Reusability: Common functionalities are defined once in the base class and reused.

Extensibility: Derived classes can add new features or override existing ones.

Organized Code: Promotes logical hierarchy and modular programming.

By understanding base and derived classes, developers can build efficient and maintainable class hierarchies in C++.

Types of Inheritance: Single, Multiple, and Multilevel

Inheritance in C++ allows classes to derive attributes and behaviors from other classes. This mechanism supports different types of inheritance based on the relationship between the base and derived classes. Here's an overview of the three main types: Single, Multiple, and Multilevel inheritance.

1. Single Inheritance

Single inheritance involves a single base class and a single derived class. The derived class inherits all accessible members of the base class.

Characteristics:

Simplifies the class hierarchy.
Useful for extending or modifying a single class.

Example:

cpp
Copy code

```cpp
#include <iostream>
using namespace std;

class Animal { // Base class
public:
    void eat() {
        cout << "This animal eats food." << endl;
    }
};

class Dog : public Animal { // Derived class
public:
    void bark() {
        cout << "The dog barks." << endl;
```

```
    }
};
```

```cpp
int main() {
    Dog myDog;
    myDog.eat(); // Inherited from Animal
    myDog.bark(); // Specific to Dog
    return 0;
}
```

Output:

Copy code
This animal eats food.
The dog barks.

2. Multiple Inheritance

Multiple inheritance involves a derived class inheriting from two or more base classes. This allows the derived class to combine the functionalities of multiple base classes.

Characteristics:

Provides a way to merge features of multiple classes.
Can lead to ambiguity if two base classes have members
with the same name (resolved using the scope resolution
operator).

Example:

```cpp
Copy code
#include <iostream>
using namespace std;

class Engine {
public:
  void startEngine() {
    cout << "Engine started." << endl;
  }
};

class Wheels {
public:
```

```cpp
    void roll() {
        cout << "Wheels are rolling." << endl;
    }
};


class Car : public Engine, public Wheels {  // Multiple inheritance
public:
    void drive() {
        cout << "Car is driving." << endl;
    }
};


int main() {
    Car myCar;
    myCar.startEngine(); // From Engine
    myCar.roll();        // From Wheels
    myCar.drive();       // From Car
    return 0;
}
```
Output:

csharp

Copy code
Engine started.
Wheels are rolling.
Car is driving.

Note: Multiple inheritance should be used cautiously to avoid the diamond problem and excessive complexity.

3. Multilevel Inheritance

Multilevel inheritance involves a chain of inheritance, where a class inherits from a derived class, forming a hierarchy.

Characteristics:

Represents a real-world hierarchical relationship.
Allows further extension of functionalities down the chain.

Example:

```cpp
cpp
Copy code
#include <iostream>
using namespace std;

class Vehicle { // Base class
public:
    void start() {
        cout << "Vehicle started." << endl;
    }
};

class Car : public Vehicle {  // Intermediate derived
class
public:
    void drive() {
        cout << "Car is driving." << endl;
    }
};

class ElectricCar : public Car { // Derived class
public:
    void charge() {
```

```cpp
        cout << "Electric car is charging." << endl;
    }
};

int main() {
    ElectricCar myCar;
    myCar.start();  // Inherited from Vehicle
    myCar.drive();  // Inherited from Car
    myCar.charge(); // Specific to ElectricCar
    return 0;
}
```
Output:

csharp
Copy code
Vehicle started.
Car is driving.
Electric car is charging.

Summary of Inheritance Types

Type	Description	Example		
Single	One derived class inherits from one base class. Dog inherits from	Dog inherits from Animal		
Multiple	One derived class inherits from multiple base classes.	Car inherits from Engine and Wheels		
Multilevel	A derived class	Electric Car inherits		

	inherits from another derived class.	from Car, which inherits from Vehicle.		

Understanding and choosing the appropriate type of inheritance ensures the development of structured, reusable, and maintainable code.

Constructor and Destructor Inheritance

In C++, constructors and destructors are special member functions responsible for initializing and cleaning up objects. When inheritance is introduced, constructors and destructors play a crucial role in ensuring proper setup and teardown of both base and derived class objects.

Constructors in Inheritance

Constructors of the base class are not inherited by the derived class. However, the base class constructor is automatically invoked when an object of the derived class is created. This ensures that the base class is properly initialized before the derived class.

Key Points:

Order of Execution: The base class constructor is called first, followed by the derived class constructor.

Explicit Constructor Calls: A derived class constructor can explicitly invoke a specific base class constructor using an initializer list.

Default Constructor: If no base class constructor is explicitly called, the default constructor of the base class is invoked.

Example:

```cpp
Copy code
#include <iostream>
using namespace std;

class Base {
public:
  Base() {
    cout << "Base class constructor called." << endl;
  }
};

class Derived : public Base {
public:
  Derived() {
        cout << "Derived class constructor called." <<
endl;
  }
};

int main() {
  Derived obj;
  return 0;
```

}

Output:

kotlin

Copy code

Base class constructor called.

Derived class constructor called.

Explicit Constructor Call:

cpp

Copy code

```
class Base {
public:
    Base(int x) {
        cout << "Base class constructor with value: " << x << endl;
    }
};


class Derived : public Base {
public:
    Derived(int x, int y) : Base(x) { // Calling base class constructor
```

```cpp
        cout << "Derived class constructor with value: " <<
y << endl;
    }
};

int main() {
    Derived obj(10, 20);
    return 0;
}
```

Output:

kotlin
Copy code
Base class constructor with value: 10
Derived class constructor with value: 20
Destructors in Inheritance

When an object of a derived class is destroyed, destructors are executed in reverse order of the constructors:

The derived class destructor is called first.

The base class destructor is called next.

This ensures that resources allocated by the derived class are cleaned up before those of the base class.

Key Points:

Automatic Invocation: Destructors are called automatically during object destruction.
Order of Execution: Destructors of the base class are called after the destructors of the derived class.

Example:

```cpp
Copy code
#include <iostream>
using namespace std;

class Base {
public:
    ~Base() {
        cout << "Base class destructor called." << endl;
```

```cpp
    }
};

class Derived : public Base {
public:
  ~Derived() {
    cout << "Derived class destructor called." << endl;
  }
};

int main() {
  Derived obj;
  return 0;
}
```

Output:

kotlin

Copy code

Derived class destructor called.

Base class destructor called.

Virtual Destructors

When a base class has a virtual destructor, it ensures that the derived class destructor is called first, even when a base class pointer points to a derived class object. This prevents resource leaks.

Example:

```cpp
Copy code
class Base {
public:
    virtual ~Base() { // Virtual destructor
        cout << "Base class destructor called." << endl;
    }
};

class Derived : public Base {
public:
    ~Derived() {
        cout << "Derived class destructor called." << endl;
    }
};
```

```
int main() {
    Base* obj = new Derived();
    delete obj;
    return 0;
}
```

Output:

kotlin

Copy code

Derived class destructor called.

Base class destructor called.

Summary

Aspect	Constructor	Destructor	
Inheritance	Not inherited; must be explicitly invoked.	Automatically invoked during object cleanup.	

Execution Order	Base class → Derived class.	Derived class → Base class.	
Virtual	Not applicable	Essential to ensure proper cleanup in polymorphism.	

Proper use of constructors and destructors in inheritance ensures that objects are initialized and destroyed safely and efficiently.

Accessing Base Class Members

In C++, when a class is derived from a base class, the derived class can access the base class members depending on their access specifiers (public, protected, or private). The accessibility rules ensure encapsulation and control over how data and functions from the base class are used or modified in the derived class.

Access Specifiers and Accessibility

Public Members:

Public members of the base class remain accessible in the derived class and to objects of the derived class.
These members can be accessed using an object of the derived class or directly within the derived class.

Protected Members:

Protected members of the base class are accessible only within the derived class and cannot be accessed by objects of the derived class.

Private Members:

Private members of the base class are not directly accessible in the derived class.

However, private members can be accessed through public or protected member functions of the base class.

Example:

Base Class Access with Public and Protected Members:

```cpp
Copy code
#include <iostream>
using namespace std;

class Base {
public:
    int publicVar;
protected:
    int protectedVar;
private:
    int privateVar;
```

```cpp
public:
    Base() : publicVar(1), protectedVar(2), privateVar(3) {}

    int getPrivateVar() { // Accessor for privateVar
        return privateVar;
    }
};

class Derived : public Base {
public:
    void showMembers() {
        cout << "Public Variable: " << publicVar << endl;
        cout << "Protected Variable: " << protectedVar << endl;
        // cout << privateVar;  // Error: privateVar is not accessible.
        cout << "Private Variable via Function: " << getPrivateVar() << endl;
    }
};

int main() {
    Derived obj;
```

```
    obj.showMembers();
    return 0;
}
```

Output:

vbnet
Copy code
Public Variable: 1
Protected Variable: 2
Private Variable via Function: 3

Access Based on Inheritance Type

The accessibility of base class members in the derived class also depends on the type of inheritance used (public, protected, or private).

Example: Public Inheritance
cpp
Copy code
class Base {
public:
    int publicVar = 10;

```cpp
protected:
    int protectedVar = 20;
private:
    int privateVar = 30;
};


class Derived : public Base {
public:
    void show() {
        cout << "Public: " << publicVar << endl;      // Accessible
        cout << "Protected: " << protectedVar << endl; // Accessible
        // cout << privateVar; // Error: privateVar is not accessible
    }
};
```

Member in Base Class	Access in Derived	Access	

	Class	Outside Derived Class	
Public	Accessible	Not Accessible	
Protected	Not Accessible	Not Accessible	

Accessing Base Class Methods

Base class methods (both public and protected) are accessible in the derived class. These methods can be overridden or explicitly called using the scope resolution operator (::).

Example: Explicit Base Class Method Call

cpp
Copy code
class Base {
public:

```cpp
   void display() {
      cout << "Base class display function" << endl;
   }
};


class Derived : public Base {
public:
   void display() {
      cout << "Derived class display function" << endl;
   }


   void callBaseDisplay() {
      Base::display();  // Explicit call to base class display
   }
};


int main() {
   Derived obj;
   obj.display();        // Calls Derived's display
   obj.callBaseDisplay(); // Calls Base's display
   return 0;
}
```

Output:

```javascript
Derived class display function
Base class display function
```

Using super-like Behavior in C++

C++ does not have a super keyword, but the base class name can be used to access base class members explicitly.

Example: Accessing Hidden Base Class Members

```cpp
class Base {
public:
    int value = 10;
};

class Derived : public Base {
```

```cpp
public:
    int value = 20;

    void show() {
        cout << "Derived value: " << value << endl;
        cout << "Base value: " << Base::value << endl; // Explicit base member access
    }
};

int main() {
    Derived obj;
    obj.show();
    return 0;
}
```

Output:

```yaml
Copy code
Derived value: 20
Base value: 10
```

Access Modifiers Recap

Specifier	Access in Derived Class)	Access Outside (Through Object	
Public	Yes	Yes	
Protected	Yes	No	
Private	No	No	

Summary

Members of a base class are accessible in the derived class based on their access specifiers.

Public and protected members can be directly accessed, while private members require accessor functions.

Base class methods can be explicitly called using the base class name and the scope resolution operator.

Proper understanding of access control ensures effective use of inheritance and encapsulation in C++.

CHAPTER 6

Polymorphism and Dynamic Binding

Polymorphism allows objects of different classes to be treated as objects of a common base class, enabling code reusability and flexibility. It comes in two forms:

Compile-Time (Static) Polymorphism: Achieved through function overloading and operator overloading.
Run-Time (Dynamic) Polymorphism: Implemented using inheritance and virtual functions.

Dynamic Binding

Dynamic binding, also known as late binding, resolves the method to be invoked at runtime rather than compile time. It is the core mechanism enabling run-time polymorphism.

Achieved using virtual functions in the base class.
Allows a derived class to override a base class method.

Example:

cpp

Copy code

```cpp
#include <iostream>
using namespace std;

class Base {
public:
    virtual void show() { // Virtual function
        cout << "Base class show() function" << endl;
    }
};

class Derived : public Base {
public:
    void show() override { // Override base class method
        cout << "Derived class show() function" << endl;
    }
};

int main() {
    Base* basePtr;
    Derived obj;
```

```cpp
    basePtr = &obj;

    basePtr->show(); // Dynamic binding: calls Derived's
show()
    return 0;
}
```

Output:

csharp
Copy code
Derived class show() function

Key Benefits:

Promotes code extensibility by allowing behavior to be defined at runtime.

Supports object-oriented principles like inheritance and polymorphism effectively.

Dynamic binding ensures flexibility and robust design in C++ applications, especially when dealing with polymorphic behavior.

Function Overloading and Operator Overloading

Both function overloading and operator overloading are examples of compile-time polymorphism, where a function or operator behaves differently based on the provided arguments or context.

Function Overloading
Function overloading allows multiple functions with the same name but different parameter lists to coexist. The compiler differentiates these functions based on the number, type, or order of arguments (known as the function's signature).

Example: Function Overloading

```cpp
Copy code
#include <iostream>
using namespace std;

class Calculator {
```

```cpp
public:
    int add(int a, int b) {
        return a + b;
    }

    double add(double a, double b) {
        return a + b;
    }

    int add(int a, int b, int c) {
        return a + b + c;
    }
};

int main() {
    Calculator calc;
    cout << "Sum (int, int): " << calc.add(5, 10) << endl;
    cout << "Sum (double, double): " << calc.add(5.5, 10.3) << endl;
    cout << "Sum (int, int, int): " << calc.add(5, 10, 15) << endl;
    return 0;
}
```

Output:

```sql
Sum (int, int): 15
Sum (double, double): 15.8
Sum (int, int, int): 30
```

Operator Overloading

Operator overloading allows developers to redefine the way operators work for user-defined types (e.g., classes). This enhances the intuitive use of operators for custom objects.

Syntax:

The keyword operator is followed by the operator to be overloaded, and the function is defined as a member or friend function.

Example: Operator Overloading

```cpp
```

```cpp
#include <iostream>
using namespace std;

class Complex {
    double real, imag;

public:
    Complex(double r = 0, double i = 0) : real(r), imag(i) {}

    // Overloading the '+' operator
    Complex operator+(const Complex& other) {
            return Complex(real + other.real, imag +
other.imag);
    }

    void display() {
        cout << real << " + " << imag << "i" << endl;
    }
};

int main() {
    Complex c1(3.5, 2.5), c2(1.5, 4.5);
    Complex c3 = c1 + c2;  // Uses overloaded '+'
```

c3.display();

return 0;

}

Output:

go

Copy code

5 + 7i

Key Differences

Aspect	Function Overloading	Operator Overloading	
Purpose	Allow Multiple Functions with the same Name	Customize Operator Behavior for user define purpose	
Scope	Functions Only	Applies to Operators	

		Like +,-,* Etc	
Flexibility	Focused on varying parameter types and counts.	Extends the functionalit y of operators	

Advantages

Function Overloading:

Improves code readability.
Reduces the need for multiple function names performing similar tasks.

Operator Overloading:

Makes custom types behave like built-in types.
Simplifies complex operations on objects.

Function and operator overloading enhance the flexibility and expressiveness of C++ programming, making it easier to work with custom types and operations.

Virtual Functions and Late Binding

Virtual functions in C++ enable run-time polymorphism, allowing derived class methods to override base class methods. This mechanism is tied to late binding (or dynamic binding), where the function to be called is determined at runtime rather than at compile time.

What Are Virtual Functions?

Declared using the keyword virtual in the base class. Allows derived classes to override the function with their own implementation.

When a base class pointer or reference points to a derived class object, the derived class's version of the function is invoked at runtime.

Late Binding

Also known as dynamic binding.
Function calls are resolved at runtime based on the object type, not the pointer or reference type.
Achieved through the use of virtual tables (vtables) and vtable pointers internally by the compiler.

Example: Virtual Functions
cpp
Copy code
#include <iostream>
using namespace std;

class Base {
public:
    virtual void display() { // Virtual function
        cout << "Base class display() function" << endl;

```
    }
};

class Derived : public Base {
public:
    void display() override {  // Override base class
method
    cout << "Derived class display() function" << endl;
  }
};

int main() {
  Base* basePtr;
  Derived obj;

  basePtr = &obj;

  basePtr->display();  // Late binding: calls Derived's
display()
  return 0;
}
```

Output:

csharp

Copy code

Derived class display() function

Key Characteristics of Virtual Functions

Declared in Base Class:

Use virtual to indicate the function can be overridden.

Defined in Derived Class:

Derived classes can provide a custom implementation.
Called Through Base Class Pointers or
References:

Ensures that the derived class's version is called during runtime.
Not Applicable for Static or Friend Functions:

Virtual functions cannot be static or friend functions.

Pure Virtual Functions

A pure virtual function is declared by assigning = 0 in the base class.

Makes the base class abstract, meaning it cannot be instantiated.

Ensures derived classes provide an implementation.
Example:

cpp
Copy code

```cpp
class Shape {
public:
    virtual void draw() = 0; // Pure virtual function
};

class Circle : public Shape {
public:
    void draw() override {
        cout << "Drawing Circle" << endl;
    }
};
```

```
int main() {
    Shape* shape = new Circle();
    shape->draw();  // Calls Circle's draw()
    delete shape;
    return 0;
}
```
Output:

mathematica
Copy code
Drawing Circle

Advantages of Virtual Functions and Late Binding

Flexibility:

Enables runtime decisions for function calls.

Extensibility:

Makes it easier to add new derived classes without modifying base class logic.

Polymorphism:

Supports a key principle of object-oriented programming.

Common Pitfalls
Performance Overhead:

Virtual functions add a slight runtime overhead due to vtable lookups.

Slicing Problem:

Ensure to use pointers or references to avoid slicing, where the derived class's data or methods are ignored.

Object Destruction:

Always declare destructors as virtual in base classes to avoid memory leaks when deleting derived class objects through base class pointers.

Conclusion

Virtual functions and late binding are critical for implementing dynamic behavior in C++ applications, enabling robust and scalable designs that adapt at runtime.

Abstract Classes and Pure Virtual Functions

Abstract classes and pure virtual functions are foundational concepts in object-oriented programming (OOP) with C++. They facilitate the creation of a blueprint for derived classes, ensuring consistency and promoting code reusability.

Abstract Classes

An abstract class is a class that cannot be instantiated directly. It is primarily used as a base class to define a common interface for derived classes.

Characteristics of Abstract Classes:

Contains at least one pure virtual function.

May include regular (non-virtual) member functions and member variables.

Serves as a template for its derived classes.

Pure Virtual Functions

A pure virtual function is a virtual function that is declared in a base class but must be overridden in derived classes. It is declared using = 0 syntax.

Syntax:

```cpp
Copy code
class AbstractBase {
public:
    virtual void pureVirtualFunction() = 0;  // Pure virtual function
};
```

When a class contains at least one pure virtual function, it becomes an abstract class.

Example: Abstract Class with Pure Virtual Function

```cpp
Copy code
#include <iostream>
using namespace std;

class Shape { // Abstract class
public:
    virtual void draw() = 0;  // Pure virtual function
    virtual ~Shape() {} // Virtual destructor
};

class Circle : public Shape {
public:
    void draw() override {
        cout << "Drawing Circle" << endl;
    }
};
```

```cpp
class Rectangle : public Shape {
public:
    void draw() override {
        cout << "Drawing Rectangle" << endl;
    }
};

int main() {
    Shape* shape1 = new Circle();
    Shape* shape2 = new Rectangle();

    shape1->draw(); // Calls Circle's draw()
    shape2->draw(); // Calls Rectangle's draw()

    delete shape1;
    delete shape2;

    return 0;
}
```
Output:

mathematica
Copy code

Drawing Circle

Drawing Rectangle

Key Benefits

Encapsulation of Interface:

Abstract classes define a standard interface for derived classes.

Enforcement of Overrides:

Ensures derived classes implement all pure virtual functions.

Polymorphism:

Enables runtime behavior using base class pointers or references.

Additional Notes

Virtual Destructor:

Abstract classes should define a virtual destructor to ensure proper cleanup of derived class objects.

Mix of Pure and Regular Methods:

Abstract classes can contain both pure virtual functions and regular member functions.

Multiple Inheritance:

A class can inherit from multiple abstract classes in C++, enabling complex hierarchies.

Use Cases

Defining common interfaces for unrelated classes.
Providing a base for polymorphism.
Enforcing a consistent implementation pattern across multiple derived classes.

Abstract classes and pure virtual functions promote clean, maintainable, and extensible code in object-oriented C++ applications.

Implementing Interfaces in C++

In C++, an interface is typically implemented using an abstract class that contains only pure virtual functions. This allows the derived classes to define specific implementations while adhering to a common structure or behavior.

What is an Interface?

An interface specifies a set of functions that a class must implement.

In C++, interfaces are represented by abstract classes with no data members and only pure virtual functions.

Interfaces help achieve polymorphism, code modularity, and flexibility in large projects.

Defining an Interface

An interface in C++ is created by declaring a class with only pure virtual functions.

Syntax:

cpp
Copy code
```
class InterfaceName {
public:
    virtual void function1() = 0; // Pure virtual function
    virtual void function2() = 0;
    virtual ~InterfaceName() {} // Virtual destructor
};
```

The = 0 makes a function pure virtual, and the presence of at least one pure virtual function makes the class abstract (cannot be instantiated).

Example: Implementing an Interface

cpp
Copy code

```cpp
#include <iostream>
using namespace std;

// Interface declaration
class Printable {
public:
    virtual void print() const = 0;  // Pure virtual function
    virtual ~Printable() {}       // Virtual destructor
};

// Class implementing the interface

class Document : public Printable {
public:
    void print() const override {
        cout << "Printing a document..." << endl;
    }
};

// Another class implementing the interface
class Image : public Printable {
public:
    void print() const override {
```

```cpp
        cout << "Printing an image..." << endl;
    }
};


int main() {
    Printable* doc = new Document();
    Printable* img = new Image();

    doc->print();  // Calls Document's implementation
    img->print();  // Calls Image's implementation

    delete doc;
    delete img;

    return 0;
}
```
Output:

arduino
Copy code
Printing a document...
Printing an image...

Key Points of C++ Interfaces

No Data Members:

Interfaces should not have data members. They define only behavior (via pure virtual functions).

Polymorphism:

Interfaces allow the use of base class pointers or references to access derived class implementations dynamically.

Multiple Inheritance:

A class can implement multiple interfaces using multiple inheritance.

```cpp
Copy code
class InterfaceA {
public:
```

```
  virtual void methodA() = 0;
};

class InterfaceB {
public:
  virtual void methodB() = 0;
};

class Combined : public InterfaceA, public InterfaceB
{
public:
  void methodA() override {
    cout << "Method A implementation" << endl;
  }
  void methodB() override {
    cout << "Method B implementation" << endl;
  }
};
```

Advantages of Using Interfaces

Flexibility:

Allows for changes in implementation without affecting dependent code.

Consistency:

Ensures that all implementing classes adhere to a specific contract.

Polymorphic Behavior:

Enables the use of a single interface to interact with multiple types of objects.

Supports Multiple Inheritance:

Interfaces avoid the complexity of sharing state in multiple inheritance scenarios since they lack data members.

Common Practices

Always include a virtual destructor in the interface to ensure proper cleanup of derived objects.

Use interfaces for defining plug-in architectures or modular designs where components interact through well-defined contracts.

Avoid adding implementation in interfaces to maintain the separation of interface and implementation.

Interfaces in C++ provide a robust way to define contracts between classes, ensuring consistent behavior while enabling flexibility and scalability in object-oriented designs.

CHAPTER 7

Object Slicing and Copy Semantics

Object Slicing

Object slicing occurs when an object of a derived class is assigned to an object of its base class. This causes the derived class-specific attributes and methods to be "sliced off," leaving only the base class portion.

Example:

cpp
Copy code
```cpp
#include <iostream>
using namespace std;
```

```cpp
class Base {
public:
    int baseData;
};

class Derived : public Base {
public:
    int derivedData;
};

int main() {
    Derived d;
    d.baseData = 10;
    d.derivedData = 20;

    Base b = d;  // Object slicing occurs here
    cout << b.baseData << endl;  // Accessible
    // cout << b.derivedData;    // Error: derivedData is
sliced off
    return 0;
}
```

Copy Semantics

Copy semantics define how an object is copied, either through a copy constructor or copy assignment operator.

Copy Constructor: Used during object initialization.
Copy Assignment Operator: Used to assign values between objects after initialization.

Example:

```cpp
Copy code
class MyClass {
    int data;

public:
    MyClass(int val) : data(val) {}
    MyClass(const MyClass& obj) { // Copy constructor
        data = obj.data;
    }
};
```

Avoiding Object Slicing

Use pointers or references to handle polymorphic behavior.

Declare the base class functions as virtual for proper inheritance handling.

Key Takeaway: Object slicing and improper copy semantics can lead to unintended behavior in C++, and understanding these concepts ensures robust object-oriented programming.

Understanding Object Slicing

Object slicing is a phenomenon in C++ where part of an object is "sliced off" when an instance of a derived class is assigned to an instance of its base class. This happens because the base class object can only hold the data and functionality defined in the base class, and any additional attributes or methods from the derived class are discarded.

How Object Slicing Occurs

When a derived class object is copied or assigned to a base class object, only the base class portion of the derived class object is retained. This happens because the compiler treats the assignment as if it were dealing with a base class object, ignoring the derived class members.

Example of Object Slicing

```cpp
Copy code
#include <iostream>
using namespace std;

class Base {
public:
    int baseValue;
    void showBase() {
        cout << "Base Value: " << baseValue << endl;
    }
};
```

```cpp
class Derived : public Base {
public:
    int derivedValue;
    void showDerived() {
        cout << "Derived Value: " << derivedValue <<
endl;
    }
};

int main() {
    Derived d;
    d.baseValue = 10;
    d.derivedValue = 20;

    Base b = d;  // Object slicing occurs here
    b.showBase();
    // b.showDerived(); // Error: 'showDerived' is not part
of Base

    return 0;
}
```
Output:

```yaml
Copy code
Base Value: 10
```

In this example, derivedValue and showDerived() from the Derived class are sliced off when d is assigned to b.

How to Avoid Object Slicing

Use Pointers or References: Instead of assigning objects directly, use pointers or references to work with polymorphism and avoid slicing.

```cpp
Copy code
Base* bPtr = &d;  // No slicing occurs
bPtr->showBase();  // Accesses base class methods
```

Enable Polymorphism: Declare the base class functions as virtual to support dynamic binding.

```cpp
```

Copy code

```
class Base {
public:
  virtual void show() {
    cout << "Base show()" << endl;
  }
};


class Derived : public Base {
public:
  void show() override {
    cout << "Derived show()" << endl;
  }
};
```

Key Characteristics of Object Slicing

Loss of Derived Class Information:
Only base class attributes and methods are retained.
Compile-Time Behavior:
The slicing is determined at compile time due to static type information.
Not an Issue with Pointers or References:

Slicing only occurs when working with value semantics.

Conclusion

Object slicing limits the functionality of derived class objects when assigned to base class objects. To leverage polymorphism and avoid slicing, it's recommended to use pointers or references and enable dynamic behavior with virtual functions. This ensures derived class-specific behavior is preserved.

Copy Constructors and Assignment Operators

In C++, the copy constructor and assignment operator are fundamental tools for copying objects. They ensure that objects are copied correctly, especially when working with dynamic memory or complex data structures.

Copy Constructor

The copy constructor initializes a new object as a copy of an existing object. It is invoked when:

A new object is created from an existing object.
An object is passed by value to a function.
An object is returned by value from a function.

Syntax:
cpp
Copy code
ClassName(const ClassName& other);

Example:
cpp
Copy code
#include <iostream>
using namespace std;

```cpp
class MyClass {
    int* data;

public:
    // Constructor
    MyClass(int value) : data(new int(value)) {}

    // Copy Constructor
    MyClass(const MyClass& obj) {
        data = new int(*obj.data);  // Deep copy
        cout << "Copy Constructor Called" << endl;
    }

    // Destructor
    ~MyClass() {
        delete data;
    }

    void display() {
        cout << "Value: " << *data << endl;
    }
};
```

```
int main() {
    MyClass obj1(10);
    MyClass obj2 = obj1;  // Copy constructor called
    obj2.display();

    return 0;
}
```
Output:

sql
Copy code
Copy Constructor Called
Value: 10

Assignment Operator

The assignment operator assigns the contents of one existing object to another existing object. It is invoked when:

An already initialized object is assigned the value of another object.

Syntax:

cpp

Copy code

ClassName& operator=(const ClassName& other);

Example:

cpp

Copy code

```
#include <iostream>
using namespace std;

class MyClass {
    int* data;

public:
    // Constructor
    MyClass(int value) : data(new int(value)) {}

    // Assignment Operator
    MyClass& operator=(const MyClass& obj) {
        if (this != &obj) { // Avoid self-assignment
            delete data; // Free existing resource
            data = new int(*obj.data); // Deep copy
```

```cpp
    }
    cout << "Assignment Operator Called" << endl;
    return *this;
  }

  // Destructor
  ~MyClass() {
    delete data;
  }

  void display() {
    cout << "Value: " << *data << endl;
  }
};

int main() {
  MyClass obj1(20);
  MyClass obj2(30);
  obj2 = obj1;  // Assignment operator called
  obj2.display();

  return 0;
}
```

Output:

```vbnet
Copy code
Assignment Operator Called
Value: 20
```

Key Differences

Feature	Copy Constructor	Assignment Operator
Purpose	Creates a new object as a copy.	Assigns values to an existing object
Invocation	When an object is initialized	When using = on existing objects.
Default Behavior	Performs a shallow copy by default.	Performs a shallow copy by default.

Customization	Useful for deep copying resources.	Avoids memory leaks in resource-heavy objects.

.

.

Best Practices

Avoid Shallow Copies:

Always implement a deep copy for classes that manage dynamic memory.
Check for Self-Assignment:
Ensure the assignment operator handles obj = obj gracefully.

Rule of Three:

If your class defines a custom destructor, copy constructor, or assignment operator, you should define all three.

Conclusion

The copy constructor and assignment operator play a critical role in managing object copying in C++. Proper implementation of these ensures memory safety, avoids resource leaks, and prevents undefined behavior, especially in classes with dynamically allocated resources.

The Rule of Three (or Five) in C++

The Rule of Three (and its extension, the Rule of Five) in C++ is a best practice for designing classes that manage resources like dynamic memory, file handles, or network connections. It ensures proper copying, assignment, and cleanup of resources, avoiding common issues such as double-deletion, memory leaks, or shallow copies.

The Rule of Three

If a class requires a custom implementation for any one of the following three special member functions, it should explicitly define all three:

Destructor:

Cleans up resources when an object goes out of scope. Necessary for freeing dynamically allocated memory or closing handles.

cpp
Copy code
~ClassName();

Copy Constructor:

Defines how a new object is initialized as a copy of an existing object.

```cpp
Copy code
ClassName(const ClassName& other);
```

Copy Assignment Operator:

Defines how an existing object is assigned the value of another existing object.

```cpp
Copy code
ClassName& operator=(const ClassName& other);
```

Example of Rule of Three

```cpp
Copy code
#include <iostream>
using namespace std;

class MyClass {
    int* data;
```

```cpp
public:
  // Constructor
  MyClass(int value) : data(new int(value)) {}

  // Destructor
  ~MyClass() {
    delete data;
    cout << "Destructor Called" << endl;
  }

  // Copy Constructor
  MyClass(const MyClass& other) : data(new int(*other.data)) {
    cout << "Copy Constructor Called" << endl;
  }

  // Copy Assignment Operator
  MyClass& operator=(const MyClass& other) {
    if (this != &other) { // Avoid self-assignment
      delete data;
      data = new int(*other.data);
    }
```

```cpp
        cout << "Copy Assignment Operator Called" <<
endl;
        return *this;
    }

    void display() const { cout << "Value: " << *data <<
endl; }
};

int main() {
    MyClass obj1(10);
    MyClass obj2 = obj1;  // Copy Constructor
    obj2.display();

    MyClass obj3(20);
    obj3 = obj1;  // Copy Assignment Operator
    obj3.display();

    return 0;
}
```

Output:

sql

```
Copy code
Copy Constructor Called
Value: 10
Copy Assignment Operator Called
Value: 10
Destructor Called
Destructor Called
Destructor Called
```

The Rule of Five

With C++11 and beyond, the Rule of Three expands into the Rule of Five to account for move semantics. If a class manages resources, it should explicitly define these additional members:

Move Constructor:

Efficiently transfers resources from one object to another, leaving the source object in a valid but undefined state.

cpp

Copy code

```cpp
ClassName(ClassName&& other) noexcept;
```

Move Assignment Operator:

Transfers resources during assignment, avoiding unnecessary deep copies.

cpp
Copy code

```cpp
ClassName& operator=(ClassName&& other) noexcept;
```

Example of Rule of Five

cpp
Copy code

```cpp
#include <iostream>
using namespace std;

class MyClass {
    int* data;

public:
```

```cpp
// Constructor
MyClass(int value) : data(new int(value)) {}

// Destructor
~MyClass() { delete data; }

// Copy Constructor
MyClass(const MyClass& other) : data(new int(*other.data)) {}

// Copy Assignment Operator
MyClass& operator=(const MyClass& other) {
    if (this != &other) {
        delete data;
        data = new int(*other.data);
    }
    return *this;
}

// Move Constructor
MyClass(MyClass&& other) noexcept : data(other.data) {
    other.data = nullptr; // Transfer ownership
```

```
        }


    // Move Assignment Operator
    MyClass& operator=(MyClass&& other) noexcept {
        if (this != &other) {
            delete data;
            data = other.data;
            other.data = nullptr;
        }
        return *this;
    }


    void display() const { cout << "Value: " << (data ?
*data : 0) << endl; }
};


int main() {
    MyClass obj1(10);
    MyClass obj2 = move(obj1);  // Move Constructor
    obj2.display();

    MyClass obj3(20);
    obj3 = move(obj2);  // Move Assignment Operator
```

obj3.display();

    return 0;

}

Output:

makefile

Copy code

Value: 10

Value: 10

Key Points

The Rule of Three is essential for managing resources in pre-C++11.

The Rule of Five extends this to include move semantics introduced in C++11, ensuring efficient resource management and transfer.

When defining custom special member functions, always consider self-assignment, resource ownership, and exception safety to avoid undefined behavior.

Conclusion

The Rule of Three (or Five) ensures robust and efficient management of resources in C++. By explicitly defining these special member functions, programmers can prevent issues such as memory leaks and undefined behavior, especially in complex applications managing dynamic resources.

Memory management and resource handling are critical aspects of C++ programming, especially for applications that use dynamic memory or other system resources like file handles or network sockets.

Dynamic Memory Management

C++ provides two primary mechanisms for allocating and deallocating memory dynamically:

new and delete:

new allocates memory for objects or arrays on the heap. delete releases the memory, preventing memory leaks.

Example:

cpp
Copy code
```
int* ptr = new int(10); // Allocate memory
```

delete ptr;   **// Free memory**

Smart Pointers (C++11 and later):

Smart pointers like std::unique_ptr, std::shared_ptr, and std::weak_ptr automatically manage memory, reducing the risk of leaks and dangling pointers.

Example:

cpp
Copy code
```cpp
std::unique_ptr<int> ptr = std::make_unique<int>(10);
```

Resource Handling

C++ uses RAII (Resource Acquisition Is Initialization) to manage resources. Resources like file handles or locks are tied to object lifetimes, ensuring they are released when the object goes out of scope.

Example:

cpp

Copy code

```cpp
#include <fstream>
void writeFile() {
    std::ofstream file("example.txt");
    if (file.is_open()) {
        file << "Hello, C++!";
    } // File is automatically closed when `file` goes out of scope
}
```

Best Practices

Always match every new with delete and every new[] with delete[].

Use smart pointers to automate resource management.

Prefer RAII patterns to tie resource management to object lifetimes.

Proper memory and resource handling prevent issues like memory leaks, segmentation faults, and undefined behavior.

Dynamic Memory Allocation with new and delete

Dynamic memory allocation in C++ allows you to allocate memory at runtime, enabling the creation of flexible and efficient programs. The new and delete operators are used to manage memory on the heap manually.

Using new

The new operator allocates memory on the heap for a single object or an array of objects. It returns a pointer to the allocated memory.

Allocating a Single Object:

cpp
Copy code
```
int* ptr = new int(10);   // Allocate memory and initialize with 10
```

Allocating an Array:

cpp

Copy code

int* arr = new int[5]; // Allocate memory for an array of 5 integers

Using delete

The delete operator releases memory allocated by new. For arrays, use delete[] to ensure proper cleanup.

Deleting a Single Object:

cpp

Copy code

delete ptr; // Free memory allocated for the single object

Deleting an Array:

cpp

Copy code

delete[] arr; // Free memory allocated for the array

Example: Allocating and Deleting Memory

cpp

Copy code

```cpp
#include <iostream>
using namespace std;

int main() {
    // Allocate memory for a single integer
    int* num = new int(42);
    cout << "Value: " << *num << endl;

    // Allocate memory for an array
    int* array = new int[3]{1, 2, 3};
    for (int i = 0; i < 3; i++) {
        cout << "Array[" << i << "] = " << array[i] << endl;
    }

    // Free the allocated memory
    delete num;      // Free single object
    delete[] array;   // Free array

    return 0;
}
```

Output:

javascript
Copy code
Value: 42
Array[0] = 1
Array[1] = 2
Array[2] = 3

Best Practices

Always pair new with delete and new[] with delete[] to avoid memory leaks.

Use smart pointers (like std::unique_ptr or std::shared_ptr) instead of raw pointers to automate memory management in modern C++.

Avoid accessing memory after it is deleted to prevent undefined behavior (dangling pointers).

Common Pitfalls

Memory Leaks: Forgetting to call delete results in memory not being released.

Dangling Pointers: Using a pointer after the memory it points to is deleted.

Mismatch: Using delete for arrays instead of delete[] can lead to undefined behavior.

By carefully managing new and delete, you can effectively utilize dynamic memory while avoiding common errors.

Smart Pointers and RAII (Resource Acquisition Is Initialization)

Smart pointers and RAII are essential techniques in modern C++ programming that simplify memory management and resource handling, making code safer and more maintainable.

Smart Pointers

Smart pointers are classes in C++ that manage the lifetime of dynamically allocated objects. They automatically release resources when no longer needed, reducing the risk of memory leaks and dangling pointers.

Types of Smart Pointers

std::unique_ptr:

Exclusive ownership of a resource.
The resource is automatically released when the unique_ptr goes out of scope.
Non-copyable but movable.

cpp
Copy code
#include <memory>
std::unique_ptr<int> ptr = std::make_unique<int>(10);

std::shared_ptr:

Shared ownership of a resource.

The resource is released when the last shared_ptr managing it is destroyed.

cpp
Copy code
#include <memory>
std::shared_ptr<int> ptr1 = std::make_shared<int>(20);
std::shared_ptr<int> ptr2 = ptr1; // Shared ownership

std::weak_ptr:

A non-owning reference to a resource managed by a shared_ptr.
Prevents circular references in shared ownership.
cpp
Copy code
#include <memory>
std::shared_ptr<int> sp = std::make_shared<int>(30);
std::weak_ptr<int> wp = sp; // Does not increase reference count

RAII (Resource Acquisition Is Initialization)

RAII is a design principle where resources (e.g., memory, file handles, or locks) are tied to the lifetime of objects. Resources are acquired during object construction and released in the destructor, ensuring deterministic cleanup.

Key Features of RAII

Automatic Cleanup:

When an object goes out of scope, its destructor releases resources.
Prevents resource leaks and simplifies error handling.

Exception Safety:

Ensures resources are properly released even if exceptions are thrown.

Example of RAII
cpp
Copy code
#include <fstream>

```cpp
#include <iostream>
using namespace std;

void writeToFile() {
    ofstream file("example.txt");
    if (!file) {
        cout << "Failed to open file." << endl;
        return;
    }
    file << "Hello, RAII!" << endl;
    // File is automatically closed when `file` goes out of scope
}
```

Smart Pointers and RAII in Action
Smart pointers embody the RAII principle by managing resource lifetimes automatically.

Example: Smart Pointer with RAII

cpp
Copy code
#include <iostream>

```cpp
#include <memory>
using namespace std;

class Resource {
public:
    Resource() { cout << "Resource acquired!" << endl; }
    ~Resource() { cout << "Resource released!" << endl; }
};

void useResource() {
    std::unique_ptr<Resource> res = std::make_unique<Resource>();
    // Resource is automatically released when `res` goes
    out of scope
}

int main() {
    useResource();
    return 0;
}
```
Output:

Copy code

Resource acquired!

Resource released!

Advantages

Automatic Memory Management:
Smart pointers reduce manual new and delete usage.

Error Prevention:

Avoids common issues like memory leaks and dangling pointers.

Exception Safety:

RAII ensures resources are released even if exceptions occur.

Code Simplification:

Developers can focus on logic rather than managing resources manually.

Conclusion

Smart pointers and RAII are powerful tools in modern C++. They work together to simplify memory and resource management, improve code reliability, and make programs safer by adhering to the principle of deterministic cleanup.

Memory Leaks and How to Avoid Them

A memory leak occurs when dynamically allocated memory is not properly deallocated, leaving it inaccessible and wasting system resources. Over time, memory leaks can degrade performance or crash applications, especially in long-running programs.

Common Causes of Memory Leaks

Forgetting to Free Dynamically Allocated Memory:

Not using delete or delete[] for memory allocated with new or new[].

```cpp
Copy code
int* ptr = new int(10);
// No delete, memory is leaked
```

Unmatched Allocation and Deallocation:

Using delete instead of delete[] for arrays allocated with new[].

```cpp
Copy code
int* arr = new int[5];
delete arr;  // Undefined behavior, should use delete[]
```

Premature Exit:

Exiting a function without releasing memory.

```cpp
Copy code
```

```cpp
void allocateMemory() {
    int* ptr = new int(5);
    if (/* some condition */) return;  // Memory is leaked
    delete ptr;
}
```

Dangling Pointers:

Losing the pointer to allocated memory before releasing it.

cpp
Copy code
```cpp
int* ptr = new int(10);
ptr = nullptr;  // Memory allocated by `new int(10)` is leaked
```

Detecting Memory Leaks

Manual Code Review:

Identify new allocations and ensure corresponding delete calls.

Memory Leak Detection Tools:

Valgrind (Linux): Detects memory leaks and improper memory access.

Visual Studio Debugger: Includes built-in memory profiling tools.

AddressSanitizer: A fast memory error detector in GCC and Clang.

How to Avoid Memory Leaks

Use Smart Pointers:

Replace raw pointers with std::unique_ptr or std::shared_ptr for automatic memory management.

cpp
Copy code
```cpp
#include <memory>
std::unique_ptr<int> ptr = std::make_unique<int>(10);
// No manual delete required
```

Follow RAII Principles:

Use objects with well-defined lifetimes to manage resources, such as using std::vector instead of manually managing arrays.

Pair new with delete:

Ensure every new is followed by a delete in all possible code paths.

cpp

Copy code

```cpp
int* ptr = new int(10);
delete ptr;  // Proper cleanup
```

Avoid Manual Memory Management

Where Possible:

Use STL containers like std::vector, std::map, etc., which manage memory automatically.

cpp

Copy code

```cpp
std::vector<int> vec = {1, 2, 3}; // No need for manual allocation
```

Initialize and Reset Pointers:

Set pointers to nullptr after deleting them to avoid dangling pointers.

cpp

Copy code

```cpp
int* ptr = new int(10);
delete ptr;
ptr = nullptr; // Safe pointer
```

Test with Tools:

Regularly test code with memory analysis tools to detect leaks early in development.

Example: Avoiding Memory Leaks

Using smart pointers to avoid manual memory management:

cpp
Copy code

```cpp
#include <iostream>
#include <memory>

void process() {
    std::unique_ptr<int> ptr = std::make_unique<int>(42);  // Memory is automatically managed
    std::cout << "Value: " << *ptr << std::endl;
    // No need for delete, memory is released when `ptr` goes out of scope
}

int main() {
    process();
    return 0;
}
```

Conclusion

Memory leaks can severely impact software performance and reliability. By adopting smart pointers, following RAII principles, and using modern tools for memory management, developers can significantly reduce the risk of memory leaks and write more robust C++ programs.

Design patterns are reusable solutions to common software design problems. In C++, they provide templates to help structure code for scalability, maintainability, and efficiency. These patterns are categorized into three main types:

1. Creational Patterns

These patterns focus on object creation, ensuring flexibility and reuse.

Singleton: Ensures a class has only one instance and provides a global access point to it.

cpp
Copy code
```cpp
class Singleton {
public:
    static Singleton& getInstance() {
        static Singleton instance;
```

```
        return instance;
    }
private:
    Singleton() {}
};
```

Factory Method: Delegates object creation to subclasses based on type.

Builder: Constructs complex objects step-by-step.

2. Structural Patterns

These patterns define relationships between entities to create larger structures.

Adapter: Converts one interface into another.

Composite: Treats individual objects and compositions of objects uniformly.

Decorator: Adds functionality to objects dynamically.

3. Behavioral Patterns

These focus on communication and interaction between objects.

Observer: Allows objects to subscribe and get notified of state changes.

```cpp
Copy code
class Observer {
    virtual void update() = 0;
};
class Subject {
    std::vector<Observer*> observers;
public:
            void    attach(Observer*    obs)    {
observers.push_back(obs); }
    void notify() { for (auto obs : observers) obs->update();
}
};
```

Strategy: Enables selecting an algorithm's behavior at runtime.

Command: Encapsulates requests as objects.

Importance of Design Patterns

Improves Code Reusability: Offers tested solutions to common issues.

Enhances Maintainability: Simplifies understanding and modifying code.

Promotes Best Practices: Encourages the use of proven methodologies.

C++ provides the flexibility to implement these patterns effectively due to its support for object-oriented and generic programming.

Introduction to Design Patterns

Design patterns are standardized solutions to recurring problems in software design. They provide a template or blueprint for solving common challenges, making code more maintainable, scalable, and reusable. In C++, design patterns are particularly valuable due to the language's complexity and versatility in object-oriented and generic programming.

What Are Design Patterns?

A design pattern is not a finished piece of code but a concept or framework that developers can adapt to suit their specific problems. They represent best practices established by experienced software engineers and address challenges in areas like object creation, communication, and structure.

Why Use Design Patterns?

Reusability: Save time by using pre-existing solutions. Consistency: Promote a standard approach to solving problems.

Improved Communication: Use a shared vocabulary among developers.

Maintainability: Simplify code updates and debugging.

Types of Design Patterns

Creational Patterns: Focus on object creation while hiding instantiation details (e.g., Singleton, Factory).

Structural Patterns: Deal with object composition to simplify large systems (e.g., Adapter, Decorator).

Behavioral Patterns: Focus on interactions and responsibilities among objects (e.g., Observer, Strategy).

C++ and Design Patterns

C++'s features like polymorphism, templates, and smart pointers make it a suitable language for implementing design patterns. For example:

Templates simplify implementing patterns like Singleton.

Smart Pointers support RAII in managing resources effectively.

Conclusion

Design patterns are essential tools for writing robust and flexible C++ programs. They encapsulate tried-and-tested solutions, making them indispensable for professional software development. Understanding and implementing design patterns can greatly improve the quality of your codebase.

Singleton, Factory, and Observer Patterns

Design patterns offer standardized solutions to common problems. Here's a closer look at Singleton, Factory, and Observer patterns:

1. Singleton Pattern

The Singleton pattern ensures that a class has only one instance throughout the application and provides a global point of access to it.

Key Features:

Restricts the instantiation of a class to one object.

Provides global access to the instance.

Implementation Example:

```cpp
Copy code
class Singleton {

public:
    static Singleton& getInstance() {
        static Singleton instance;
        return instance;
    }

private:
    Singleton() {} // Constructor is private
    Singleton(const Singleton&) = delete;
    Singleton& operator=(const Singleton&) = delete;
};
```

Use Cases:

Configuration management.
Logging systems.
Database connections.

2. Factory Pattern

The Factory pattern provides a way to create objects without specifying the exact class of the object. It promotes loose coupling and flexibility by using a common interface.

Key Features:

Defines a method to create objects, allowing subclasses to alter the type of objects created.
Encapsulates object creation logic.
Implementation Example:

cpp
Copy code
class Shape {

```cpp
public:
    virtual void draw() = 0;
};

class Circle : public Shape {
public:
    void draw() override { std::cout << "Drawing Circle\n"; }
};

class Square : public Shape {
public:
    void draw() override { std::cout << "Drawing Square\n"; }
};

class ShapeFactory {
public:
    static Shape* createShape(const std::string& type) {
        if (type == "circle") return new Circle();
        if (type == "square") return new Square();
        return nullptr;
    }
```

```
};
```

Use Cases:

Creating objects where the exact class may vary at runtime.
Managing object creation in large systems.

3. Observer Pattern

The Observer pattern defines a one-to-many dependency between objects so that when one object (subject) changes state, all its dependents (observers) are notified automatically.

Key Features:

Useful for implementing event-driven systems.
Promotes loose coupling between subject and observers.

Implementation Example:

cpp

```
Copy code
#include <vector>
#include <iostream>

class Observer {
public:
    virtual void update() = 0;
};

class Subject {
private:
    std::vector<Observer*> observers;

public:
    void attach(Observer* obs) {
observers.push_back(obs); }
    void notify() {
        for (auto obs : observers) {
            obs->update();
        }
    }
};
```

```cpp
class ConcreteObserver : public Observer {
public:
    void update() override {
        std::cout << "Observer notified!\n";
    }
};

int main() {
    Subject subject;
    ConcreteObserver obs1, obs2;

    subject.attach(&obs1);
    subject.attach(&obs2);

    subject.notify(); // Notifies all observers
    return 0;
}
```

Use Cases:

GUI frameworks (e.g., updating multiple UI components when data changes).

Event-driven systems.

Comparison

Pattern	Purpose	Key Feature
Singleton	Ensure one instance of a class.	Global access point.
Factory	Encapsulate object creation.	Flexibility in object creation.
Observer	Notify multiple objects of a state change.	Event-driven communication.

These patterns are fundamental to designing scalable and maintainable C++ applications.

Strategy and Command Patterns

Both the Strategy and Command patterns are behavioral design patterns that aim to manage algorithms, relationships, and responsibilities between objects effectively. They help in writing flexible and maintainable code by separating concerns.

1. Strategy Pattern

The Strategy Pattern allows selecting an algorithm's behavior at runtime by encapsulating it within a class. It promotes the Open/Closed Principle, enabling algorithms to be extended without altering existing code.

Key Features:

Defines a family of interchangeable algorithms.
Decouples the algorithm from the context where it is used.
Simplifies adding or modifying algorithms.

Implementation Example:

```cpp
Copy code
#include <iostream>

// Strategy Interface
class SortStrategy {
public:
    virtual void sort() = 0;
};

// Concrete Strategies
class QuickSort : public SortStrategy {
public:
    void sort() override { std::cout << "QuickSort algorithm\n"; }
};

class MergeSort : public SortStrategy {
public:
```

```cpp
    void sort() override { std::cout << "MergeSort
algorithm\n"; }
};

// Context
class Context {
private:
    SortStrategy* strategy;
public:
    Context(SortStrategy* strat) : strategy(strat) {}
    void setStrategy(SortStrategy* strat) { strategy =
strat; }
    void executeStrategy() { strategy->sort(); }
};

// Usage
int main() {
    QuickSort quickSort;
    MergeSort mergeSort;

    Context context(&quickSort);
    context.executeStrategy();  // Uses QuickSort
```

```
context.setStrategy(&mergeSort);
context.executeStrategy(); // Switches to MergeSort
return 0;
}
```

Use Cases:

Sorting algorithms.

Payment processing systems with different payment methods.

Compression utilities supporting multiple formats.

2. Command Pattern

The Command Pattern encapsulates a request as an object, allowing the parameterization of clients with different requests, the queuing of requests, and logging. It decouples the sender and receiver, making the system more flexible.

Key Features:

Encapsulates commands as objects.

Supports undo/redo functionality.

Facilitates command queuing and logging.

Implementation Example:

cpp

Copy code

```cpp
#include <iostream>
#include <vector>

// Command Interface
class Command {
public:
    virtual void execute() = 0;
};

// Receiver
class Light {
public:
    void turnOn() { std::cout << "Light is ON\n"; }
    void turnOff() { std::cout << "Light is OFF\n"; }
};

// Concrete Commands
```

```cpp
class TurnOnCommand : public Command {
private:
    Light& light;
public:
    TurnOnCommand(Light& l) : light(l) {}
    void execute() override { light.turnOn(); }
};

class TurnOffCommand : public Command {
private:
    Light& light;
public:
    TurnOffCommand(Light& l) : light(l) {}
    void execute() override { light.turnOff(); }
};

// Invoker
class RemoteControl {
private:
    std::vector<Command*> commands;
public:
    void addCommand(Command* cmd) {
commands.push_back(cmd); }
```

```cpp
    void executeCommands() {
        for (auto cmd : commands) {
            cmd->execute();
        }
    }
};

// Usage
int main() {
    Light light;

    TurnOnCommand onCmd(light);
    TurnOffCommand offCmd(light);

    RemoteControl remote;
    remote.addCommand(&onCmd);
    remote.addCommand(&offCmd);

    remote.executeCommands();
    return 0;
}
```

Use Cases:

Home automation systems (e.g., controlling lights or appliances).

GUI frameworks (e.g., buttons triggering commands).

Task scheduling systems.

Comparison of Strategy and Command Patterns

Aspect Strategy	Pattern	Command Pattern
Purpose	Allows dynamic selection of algorithms.	Encapsulates actions or requests as objects.
Flexibility	Easy to switch or add algorithms.	Supports undo, redo, and queuing.

Usage Context	Algorithm selection (e.g., sorting, payment).	Task execution (e.g., GUI commands).

Both patterns encourage modular design, but they address different problems. The Strategy Pattern focuses on choosing behaviors dynamically, while the Command Pattern encapsulates operations for greater flexibility and control.

PART IV: DESIGN STRATEGIES FOR SCALABLE SOFTWARE

CHAPTER 10
Designing Modular and Scalable Systems

Modular and scalable systems are essential for managing complexity and adapting to growth in modern software development. A well-designed system ensures maintainability, flexibility, and performance under increasing demands.

Key Principles:

Modularity:

Break the system into smaller, independent modules. Each module should focus on a single responsibility and communicate via well-defined interfaces.

Scalability:

Ensure the system can handle increased workload by scaling vertically (adding resources to existing nodes) or horizontally (adding more nodes).

Decoupling:

Reduce dependencies between modules using design patterns like Dependency Injection and Observer.

Reusability:

Design components to be reusable across different parts of the system or projects.
Extensibility:

Use abstraction to allow future enhancements without altering existing code

Best Practices:

Adopt Layered Architecture: Separate concerns into layers (e.g., presentation, business logic, data access).

Use Design Patterns: Apply patterns like Factory, Singleton, and Strategy for effective module design.

Implement Testing: Ensure modules are independently testable with unit and integration tests.

Monitor and Optimize: Continuously monitor performance and refactor bottlenecks.

By adhering to these principles, you can create systems that are easy to develop, maintain, and expand.

Breaking Down Complex Systems into Modules

Breaking down complex systems into smaller, manageable modules is a core practice in software engineering. It enhances clarity, maintainability, and scalability, making it easier to design, develop, and debug large applications.

Key Steps to Modularization

Understand the System Requirements:

Identify the overall goals and features of the system.
Define boundaries and responsibilities for each component.

Identify Logical Groupings:

Divide the system based on functionality (e.g., authentication, data processing, user interface).
Group related tasks or data into cohesive units.

Define Clear Interfaces:

Establish well-defined APIs or interfaces for communication between modules.
Ensure minimal coupling between modules.

Focus on Single Responsibility:

Apply the Single Responsibility Principle (SRP): each module should handle only one aspect of functionality. This makes modules easier to understand and modify.

Encapsulate Data and Logic:

Keep implementation details private within a module. Expose only necessary functions or data to other parts of the system.

Adopt Standard Design Patterns:

Use patterns like MVC (Model-View-Controller), Factory, or Observer to structure modules effectively.

Benefits of Modularization

Simplified Development: Developers can work on individual modules without worrying about the entire system.
Improved Maintainability: Changes in one module have minimal impact on others.

Reusability: Modules can be reused across different projects or systems.

Scalability: Modules can be scaled independently based on requirements.

Parallel Development: Teams can work on different modules simultaneously, speeding up development.

Example: Modularizing a Web Application

Authentication Module: Handles login, registration, and user management.

Database Module: Manages data storage and retrieval.

API Module: Provides endpoints for client-server communication.

UI Module: Renders the user interface and handles interactions.

By modularizing complex systems, you create a structure that is easier to manage and adapt, enabling long-term success in software projects.

Layered Architecture and Separation of Concerns

Layered architecture is a design approach that divides a system into distinct layers, each with specific responsibilities. It adheres to the principle of separation of concerns (SoC), ensuring that each layer handles a unique aspect of the application. This approach improves modularity, maintainability, and scalability.

Key Layers in Layered Architecture

Presentation Layer:

Responsible for the user interface (UI) and user interactions.
Focuses on displaying data and collecting user input.

Examples: Webpages, mobile screens, or desktop GUIs.

Business Logic Layer:

Encapsulates the core application logic and rules.

Acts as a bridge between the presentation and data layers.

Example: Calculations, data validation, or decision-making.

Data Access Layer:

Handles data storage and retrieval operations.

Provides an abstraction over database operations, ensuring that the business logic layer is not directly interacting with the database.

Example: SQL queries, ORM frameworks like Hibernate.

Database Layer:

Manages the actual storage of application data.

Includes database schema, tables, and stored procedures.

Example: Relational databases like MySQL or NoSQL solutions like MongoDB.

Separation of Concerns (SoC)

SoC is a design principle that ensures each layer or component in the system addresses only a specific aspect of the functionality. This decoupling promotes clean and organized code.

Encapsulation: Each layer has its own implementation details hidden from others.
Independence: Changes in one layer (e.g., swapping the database) minimally affect other layers.

Benefits of Layered Architecture and SoC

Improved Maintainability:

Bugs or changes can be localized to a specific layer.

Reusability:
Layers, like the business logic, can be reused across different interfaces (e.g., web and mobile).

Ease of Testing:

Layers can be tested independently, simplifying debugging.

Scalability:

Individual layers can be scaled as needed.

Flexibility:

Easier to adapt to new technologies or requirements (e.g., replacing the UI or database).

Example: E-commerce Application

Presentation Layer: HTML/CSS for UI, JavaScript for interaction.
Business Logic Layer: Processes orders, calculates discounts, manages inventory.
Data Access Layer: Interfaces with a MySQL database.
Database Layer: Stores customer, product, and order information.

By leveraging layered architecture and adhering to SoC, software systems become robust, adaptable, and easier to develop and maintain over time.

Dependency Injection and Loose Coupling

Dependency Injection (DI) is a design pattern that facilitates loose coupling between software components. It involves providing an object its dependencies from an external source rather than allowing the object to create or manage its dependencies itself.

Loose coupling ensures that components or modules are minimally dependent on one another, making the system more flexible, testable, and maintainable.

What Is Dependency Injection?

Dependency Injection is a technique where objects are not responsible for instantiating their dependencies.

Instead, an external framework or container provides the required dependencies.

Example: Instead of a class creating its own database connection, it receives the connection as a dependency.

Types of Dependency Injection

Constructor Injection:

Dependencies are passed via the class constructor.

Example:

```cpp
Copy code
class Database {
public:
    Database(Logger* logger) : logger_(logger) {}
    void query() { logger_->log("Executing query"); }
private:
    Logger* logger_;
};
```

Setter Injection:

Dependencies are provided through setter methods.

Example:
cpp
Copy code

```cpp
class Database {
public:
    void setLogger(Logger* logger) { logger_ = logger; }
    void query() { logger_->log("Executing query"); }
private:
    Logger* logger_;
};
```

Interface Injection:

The dependency provides a method that the dependent class calls to inject itself.

Rare in C++ but common in other languages.

What Is Loose Coupling?

Loose coupling minimizes the interdependencies between components, allowing changes in one component without significantly affecting others. This is achieved by depending on abstractions (like interfaces) rather than concrete implementations.

Example: A Database class depends on an abstract Logger interface rather than a specific ConsoleLogger or FileLogger.

Benefits of Dependency Injection and Loose Coupling

Improved Testability:
Dependencies can be mocked or stubbed, making unit testing easier.

Enhanced Flexibility:
Components can be swapped or extended with minimal impact on the system.

Easier Maintenance:

Isolated changes are less likely to introduce cascading failures.

Better Reusability:
Components can be reused in different contexts without modification.

Implementing DI and Loose Coupling in C++

C++ does not have a built-in DI framework, but it can be implemented manually or with libraries like Boost.DI.

Manual DI Example:

```cpp
Copy code
class Logger {
public:
    virtual void log(const std::string& message) = 0;
};

class ConsoleLogger : public Logger {
public:
```

```cpp
    void log(const std::string& message) override {
        std::cout << message << std::endl;
    }
};

class Database {
public:
    Database(Logger* logger) : logger_(logger) {}
    void query() { logger_->log("Executing query"); }
private:
    Logger* logger_;
};

int main() {
    ConsoleLogger logger;
    Database db(&logger);
    db.query();
    return 0;
}
```

Dependency Injection and Loose Coupling promote modular, robust, and maintainable software, enabling developers to build systems that adapt to change and scale gracefully.

CHAPTER 11
: Writing Maintainable and Extensible Code

Maintainable and extensible code ensures long-term software success by making it easy to update, debug, and expand without disrupting existing functionality.

Principles for Maintainable Code

Clarity:

Write clean, readable code with meaningful names for variables, functions, and classes.

Use comments and documentation to explain complex logic.

Consistency:

Follow consistent coding standards and formatting throughout the project.

Modularity:

Break the code into smaller, independent modules that handle specific responsibilities.

Testing:

Write unit tests and integration tests to catch errors early and ensure reliability.

Principles for Extensible Code

Adopt SOLID Principles:

Especially Open-Closed Principle (OCP): Code should be open to extension but closed to modification.

Use Abstraction:

Leverage interfaces or abstract classes to define extensible functionality.

Employ Design Patterns:

Use patterns like Strategy, Factory, and Observer to support flexible and reusable code.

Avoid Hardcoding:

Use configuration files, constants, or environment variables for dynamic settings.

By focusing on these principles, developers can create software that is easy to maintain and adaptable to changing requirements, ensuring the system remains robust and future-proof.

Principles of Clean Code in C++

Clean code is essential for creating software that is readable, maintainable, and robust. In C++, clean code involves adhering to best practices that emphasize clarity, simplicity, and efficiency.

Key Principles of Clean Code

Meaningful Naming:

Use descriptive and precise names for variables, functions, and classes.

Example:
cpp
Copy code
```cpp
int calculateArea(int width, int height); // Clear purpose
```

Function Simplicity:

Functions should be small and perform a single task. Avoid long, multi-purpose functions.

Example:

```cpp
Copy code
void drawCircle();
void drawRectangle();
```

Consistency:

Follow consistent coding standards (e.g., indentation, braces, naming conventions) across the project.

Avoid Magic Numbers:

Use constants or enums for hardcoded values.
Example:

```cpp
Copy code
const int MAX_USERS = 100;
```

Code Modularity:

Break code into reusable components, such as classes and functions.

Each module should focus on a single responsibility.

Encapsulation:

Use access modifiers (public, private, protected) to control visibility and protect data.

Example:

```cpp
Copy code
class Account {
private:
    double balance;
public:
    void deposit(double amount);
};
```

Minimize Dependencies:

Reduce coupling between modules to simplify maintenance and testing.
Use forward declarations and avoid including unnecessary headers.

Error Handling:

Use exceptions and proper error checks to handle failures gracefully.

Example:

cpp

Copy code

```cpp
try {
    // Code that may throw exceptions
} catch (const std::exception& e) {
    std::cerr << e.what() << std::endl;
}
```

Comment Judiciously:

Write comments to explain why, not what, the code does.

Example:

cpp
Copy code
```cpp
// Adjusting price to include tax
price += price * taxRate;
```

Leverage C++ Best Practices:

Use smart pointers (std::shared_ptr, std::unique_ptr) for memory management.
Prefer modern C++ features like auto, std::vector, and range-based for loops for cleaner syntax.

Benefits of Clean Code

Improved Readability: Easier for other developers to understand and work on the code.
Reduced Technical Debt: Fewer future maintenance challenges.
Simplified Debugging: Clear structure makes identifying issues faster.

Scalability: Easier to extend with new features.

By adhering to these principles, C++ developers can ensure their codebase is efficient, maintainable, and adaptable to future requirements.

Refactoring Techniques

Refactoring is the process of improving the structure, readability, and efficiency of code without changing its external behavior. It helps maintain a clean codebase, reduces technical debt, and simplifies future development.

Key Refactoring Techniques

Rename Variables and Methods:

Choose meaningful names to improve code clarity.

Example:

cpp

Copy code

```cpp
int x; // Rename to
int totalScore;
```

Extract Method:

Break large functions into smaller, reusable functions.

Example:

cpp

Copy code

```cpp
void calculate() {
    calculateTax();
    calculateDiscount();
}
```

Inline Method:

Remove unnecessary method calls by embedding their logic directly.

Example:

cpp
Copy code
// Replace
getTaxAmount();
// With
total * taxRate;

Replace Magic Numbers with Constants:

Use descriptive constants instead of hardcoded numbers.

Example:
cpp
Copy code
const int MAX_RETRIES = 3;

Simplify Conditional Statements:

Refactor complex if-else chains or nested conditionals for readability.
Example:

```cpp
Copy code
if (status == ACTIVE) { ... }
```

Encapsulate Fields:

Use getter and setter methods to control access to class members.

Example:

```cpp
Copy code
class Account {
  private:
    double balance;
  public:
    double getBalance();
    void setBalance(double amount);
};
```

Remove Dead Code:

Delete unused or redundant variables, functions, and classes.

Consolidate Duplicated Code:

Merge repeated code into a single function or method.

Example:

cpp

Copy code

```cpp
void logMessage(const std::string& message);
```

Replace Loops with Algorithms:

Use C++ Standard Library algorithms like std::transform or std::for_each.

Example:

cpp

Copy code

```cpp
std::transform(vec.begin(), vec.end(), vec.begin(), [](int x) { return x * 2; });
```

Introduce Design Patterns:

Apply patterns like Singleton, Factory, or Strategy to simplify and structure the code.

Refactoring Workflow

Analyze: Identify areas with poor readability, performance, or design.

Plan: Choose appropriate techniques and ensure the functionality remains intact.

Test: Implement changes iteratively, testing thoroughly at each step.

Optimize: Refactor for performance after ensuring code correctness.

Benefits of Refactoring

Improved Code Quality: Enhances readability, maintainability, and efficiency.

Reduced Complexity: Simplifies overly complicated code structures.

Enhanced Reusability: Modularizes code for easier reuse.

Future-Proofing: Prepares the codebase for easier feature addition and debugging.

By applying these refactoring techniques, developers can transform a cluttered codebase into a clean, efficient, and scalable system.

Test-Driven Development (TDD) in OOP

Test-Driven Development (TDD) is a software development approach where tests are written before the actual implementation of the code. In Object-Oriented Programming (OOP), TDD helps ensure that classes, objects, and their interactions work as intended, promoting better design and maintainable code.

Key Principles of TDD

Write Tests First:

Begin by writing test cases that define the desired functionality.

Fail the Test:

Ensure the test fails initially to validate its correctness.

Write Minimal Code:

Implement just enough code to pass the test.

Refactor:

Improve the code structure without altering its behavior.

Repeat:

Add new tests for additional functionality and repeat the cycle.

TDD Process in OOP

Identify Requirements:

Define the functionality for a specific class or method.

Write a Test:

Use a testing framework (e.g., Google Test or Catch2 for C++).

Example:

cpp
Copy code

```cpp
TEST(AccountTest, BalanceCheck) {
    Account account;
    EXPECT_EQ(account.getBalance(), 0);
}
```

Run the Test:

Confirm that the test fails, indicating the feature is not yet implemented.

Implement Code:

Write the class or method to fulfill the test requirement.

Example:

cpp
Copy code

```
class Account {
private:
    double balance = 0.0;
public:
    double getBalance() { return balance; }
};
```

Run Tests Again:

Ensure the test passes after the implementation.
Refactor:

Clean up the code without changing its functionality.

Benefits of TDD in OOP

Improved Design:

Encourages designing classes and methods with clear responsibilities.

Early Bug Detection:

Issues are identified and resolved during the development phase.

Maintainable Code:
Well-tested code is easier to modify and extend.

Confidence in Code:
Developers can make changes knowing the tests validate the behavior.

TDD Best Practices

Test Granularity:

Write small, focused tests for individual classes or methods.

Mocking and Stubbing:

Use mocks to test class interactions without relying on actual implementations.

Follow SOLID Principles:

Ensure objects and their dependencies are well-structured for easy testing.

Automate Testing:
Automate the test suite to quickly verify changes.

By integrating TDD with OOP, developers can create robust, maintainable, and well-tested systems that align with user requirements and are easy to adapt to future changes.

CHAPTER 12
Optimizing Object Creation and Destruction

Efficient object creation and destruction are crucial for performance and resource management in C++. Proper optimization ensures reduced overhead and better memory usage.

Best Practices for Optimization

Use Constructors and Destructors Wisely:

Initialize member variables in constructors.
Release resources (e.g., dynamic memory or file handles) in destructors.

Example:

cpp
Copy code
```cpp
class Resource {
private:
```

```cpp
    int* data;
public:
    Resource() : data(new int[100]) {}
    ~Resource() { delete[] data; }
};
```

Avoid Unnecessary Object Copies:

Use move semantics (introduced in C++11) for efficient object transfers.

Example:
cpp
Copy code
```cpp
std::vector<int> v1 = {1, 2, 3};
std::vector<int> v2 = std::move(v1); // Avoids copying
```

Implement Copy Constructor and Assignment Operator:

Follow the Rule of Three (or Five) to manage resources effectively when copying or assigning objects.

Example:

cpp

Copy code

```cpp
Resource(const Resource& other) = delete; // Disable copying if not needed
```

Use Smart Pointers:

Use std::unique_ptr or std::shared_ptr to manage dynamic memory automatically.

Example:

cpp

Copy code

```cpp
std::unique_ptr<int> ptr(new int(5));
```

Leverage Object Pools:

Reuse pre-allocated objects to reduce creation/destruction overhead in performance-critical applications.

Inline Small Functions:

Use the inline keyword for frequently called, small functions to avoid function call overhead.

Minimize Dynamic Allocations:

Prefer stack allocation over heap allocation whenever possible for better performance.

Example:
cpp
Copy code
int arr[100]; // Stack allocation

Use Defaulted or Deleted Special Member Functions:

Explicitly default or delete constructors and destructors when applicable to optimize behavior.

Example:

cpp
Copy code
class NonCopyable {

public:

    NonCopyable() = default;

    NonCopyable(const NonCopyable&) = delete;

      NonCopyable& operator=(const NonCopyable&) =
delete;

};

By employing these techniques, you can optimize the lifecycle of objects, leading to faster execution and better resource utilization in C++ applications.

Reducing Overhead in Object Construction

Efficient object construction is critical for optimizing performance, especially in large-scale or performance-critical applications. Reducing overhead ensures that object creation is fast and consumes minimal resources.

Techniques to Reduce Overhead

Use Member Initializer Lists:

Initialize member variables in the constructor initializer list to avoid redundant assignments.

Example:

cpp

Copy code

```cpp
class MyClass {
    int x;
public:
    MyClass(int value) : x(value) {} // Direct initialization
};
```

Avoid Expensive Operations in Constructors:

Minimize heavy computations or I/O operations during object construction. Defer them until they are necessary.

Prefer Lazy Initialization:

Initialize expensive resources only when they are needed.

Example:

cpp

Copy code

```cpp
class LazyInit {
    std::unique_ptr<int> data;
public:
    int getData() {
        if (!data) data = std::make_unique<int>(100);
        return *data;
    }
};
```

Leverage Move Semantics:

Use move constructors and move assignment operators to transfer resources instead of copying them.

Example:

cpp

Copy code

```cpp
std::vector<int> vec1 = {1, 2, 3};
```

```cpp
std::vector<int> vec2 = std::move(vec1); // Efficient
resource transfer
```

Reuse Objects via Object Pools:

Use object pools to recycle existing objects instead of creating and destroying them repeatedly.
Common in real-time systems or game engines.

Use Default Constructors When Possible:

Avoid custom constructors if default behavior suffices.
Example:
cpp
Copy code
```cpp
struct Simple {
    int x = 0;
    double y = 0.0; // Default initialization
};
```

Minimize Dynamic Memory Allocation:

Use stack allocation or fixed-size containers to reduce heap allocation overhead.

Example:

cpp
Copy code
```
int arr[100]; // Faster than dynamic allocation
```

Inline Constructor Code:

For simple constructors, use inline definitions to eliminate function call overhead.

Example:
cpp
Copy code
```
class InlineExample {
    int x;
public:
    InlineExample(int value) : x(value) {} // Inline constructor
};
```

Avoid Virtual Functions in Frequently Constructed

Classes:

Avoid adding virtual functions to classes that are instantiated frequently, as it increases memory and initialization overhead.

Use Aggregate Initialization:

Take advantage of aggregate initialization for structs and classes without explicit constructors.

Example:

```cpp
Copy code
struct Data {
    int x;
    double y;
};
Data d = {10, 20.5}; // Aggregate initialization
```

Benefits of Optimizing Object Construction

Improved Performance:

Faster object creation leads to reduced application latency.

Efficient Resource Usage:

Minimizes unnecessary memory and CPU consumption.
Scalability:
Makes the application capable of handling larger workloads efficiently.

By applying these techniques, developers can significantly reduce the overhead associated with object construction and achieve better performance in C++ applications.

Object Pooling Techniques

Object pooling is a design pattern used to optimize resource utilization by reusing objects rather than creating and destroying them repeatedly. This technique is particularly useful in scenarios where object creation and destruction are expensive operations, such as in real-time systems, game development, or network applications.

How Object Pooling Works
Object Preallocation:

A fixed number of objects are created and stored in a pool at the start of the application.

Object Reuse:

When a new object is required, it is taken from the pool rather than being created anew.

Return to Pool:

Once the object is no longer needed, it is reset to a clean state and returned to the pool for reuse.

Advantages of Object Pooling

Improved Performance:

Reduces the overhead of frequent memory allocation and deallocation.

Efficient Resource Management:

Limits the number of objects in use, preventing excessive memory consumption.

Reduced Garbage Collection:

Minimizes the impact of garbage collection in systems like managed environments.

Implementation Steps

Create a Pool Manager:

A class that manages the lifecycle of pooled objects.

Initialize the Pool:
Preallocate a specified number of objects.

Provide Object Access:

Methods to acquire and release objects from the pool.

Reset Objects:
Ensure objects are reset to a default state before reuse.

Example in C++
cpp
Copy code

```cpp
#include <vector>
#include <memory>

class Object {
public:
  void reset() {
    // Reset object state
  }
```

```cpp
};

class ObjectPool {
private:
  std::vector<std::unique_ptr<Object>> pool;
  size_t poolSize;

public:
  ObjectPool(size_t size) : poolSize(size) {
    for (size_t i = 0; i < size; ++i) {

pool.emplace_back(std::make_unique<Object>());
    }
  }

  std::unique_ptr<Object> acquire() {
    if (!pool.empty()) {
                      std::unique_ptr<Object> obj =
std::move(pool.back());
      pool.pop_back();
      return obj;
    }
```

```cpp
        return std::make_unique<Object>(); // Create new
if pool is empty
    }

    void release(std::unique_ptr<Object> obj) {
        obj->reset();
        pool.push_back(std::move(obj));
    }
};
```

Best Practices

Determine Pool Size:

Choose a pool size based on expected workload to balance memory usage and availability.

Thread Safety:

Use synchronization mechanisms like mutexes if the pool is accessed by multiple threads.

Avoid Overuse:

Use object pooling only for frequently reused objects with high creation/destruction costs.

Monitor Pool Usage:
Implement metrics to track pool utilization and resize if necessary.

Applications of Object Pooling

Game Development:
Managing bullets, enemies, or other game objects.

Networking:
Reusing connection or packet objects in high-frequency applications.

Database Connection Management:
Pooling database connections to reduce latency.

By implementing object pooling techniques, developers can achieve significant performance improvements and optimize resource handling in their C++ applications.

Inheritance and polymorphism are key features of Object-Oriented Programming (OOP) that enable code reuse and flexibility. Efficient use of these principles ensures maintainable and high-performance applications.

Best Practices for Inheritance

Favor Composition Over Inheritance:

Use inheritance only when there is a clear "is-a" relationship.
Prefer composition to reuse functionality without tightly coupling classes.

Minimize Inheritance Depth:

Avoid deep inheritance hierarchies to reduce complexity and improve readability.

Use Protected Members Judiciously:

Expose only the necessary members to derived classes to maintain encapsulation.

Leverage Virtual Inheritance:

Prevent the diamond problem in multiple inheritance by using virtual inheritance.

Example:
cpp
Copy code
```cpp
class Base {};
class Derived1 : virtual public Base {};
class Derived2 : virtual public Base {};
```

Best Practices for Polymorphism

Use Virtual Functions for Flexibility:

Enable dynamic behavior through function overriding.

Example:

cpp
Copy code

```cpp
class Base {
public:
    virtual void display() { std::cout << "Base" << std::endl; }
};
class Derived : public Base {
public:
    void display() override { std::cout << "Derived" << std::endl; }
};
```

Avoid Virtual Function Overhead When Not Needed:

Use final for classes or methods to avoid unnecessary polymorphism.
Example:

cpp
Copy code
```cpp
class FinalClass final {};
```

Use Smart Pointers for Polymorphic Objects:

Manage polymorphic objects with std::shared_ptr or std::unique_ptr for safer memory handling.
Prefer Abstract Base Classes for Interfaces:

Use pure virtual functions to define interfaces for flexibility and extendability.

Example:
cpp
Copy code
```cpp
class Interface {
public:
    virtual void execute() = 0;
    virtual ~Interface() {}
};
```

Benefits of Efficient Use

Code Reusability: Reduces redundancy and improves maintainability.

Extensibility: Simplifies adding new features without modifying existing code.

Performance Optimization: Minimizes unnecessary overhead from misuse of polymorphism or deep inheritance chains.

By applying these principles effectively, developers can create robust, scalable, and efficient systems.

Avoiding Performance Pitfalls in Inheritance

While inheritance is a powerful feature of Object-Oriented Programming (OOP), it can lead to performance issues if not used carefully. Avoiding common pitfalls ensures both efficient and maintainable code.

Key Performance Pitfalls and Solutions

Unnecessary Virtual Functions:

Pitfall: Overuse of virtual functions can introduce runtime overhead due to dynamic dispatch.
Solution: Use virtual functions only when polymorphism is required. Mark functions with final if overriding is not needed.

Example:

```cpp
Copy code
class Base {
public:
    virtual void process() { /* Default implementation */ }
};
class Derived final : public Base {
public:
```

```cpp
    void process() override final { /* Custom
implementation */ }
};
```

Deep Inheritance Hierarchies:

Pitfall: Excessively deep hierarchies increase code complexity and slow down execution due to multiple pointer traversals.
Solution: Keep hierarchies shallow and use composition for code reuse where possible.

Excessive Use of Virtual Base Classes:

Pitfall: Virtual inheritance can cause extra overhead by maintaining additional pointers to handle base class ambiguities.
Solution: Use virtual inheritance only when resolving the diamond problem in multiple inheritance.

Example:

cpp

```
Copy code
class Base {};
class Derived1 : virtual public Base {};
class Derived2 : virtual public Base {};
class Final : public Derived1, public Derived2 {};
```

Object Slicing:

Pitfall: Copying or assigning derived objects to base class objects slices off derived class-specific data, leading to data loss and unexpected behavior.

Solution: Always use pointers or references to base classes when dealing with polymorphism.

Example:

cpp
Copy code
```
class Base {
public:
    virtual void display() const { /* Base logic */ }
};
class Derived : public Base {
```

public:
  void display() const override { /* Derived logic */ }
};
void show(const Base& obj) { obj.display(); } // Avoid slicing

Improper Destructor Design:

Pitfall: Not declaring destructors as virtual in base classes can lead to resource leaks when deleting derived objects via base class pointers.
Solution: Declare destructors in base classes as virtual to ensure proper cleanup.

Example:

```cpp
Copy code
class Base {
public:
   virtual ~Base() { /* Cleanup resources */ }
};
```

Additional Tips for Avoiding Pitfalls

Use Static Polymorphism When Possible:

Leverage templates and compile-time polymorphism to avoid the runtime cost of dynamic dispatch.

Avoid Excessive Downcasting:

Use dynamic_cast sparingly as it adds runtime overhead. Redesign the hierarchy to minimize the need for casting.

Profile and Optimize:

Use profiling tools to identify inheritance-related bottlenecks and refactor accordingly.

Benefits of Avoiding Pitfalls

Improved Performance: Reduces unnecessary runtime overhead.
Cleaner Design: Encourages maintainable and comprehensible class structures.

Enhanced Scalability: Ensures the application remains efficient as complexity grows.

By adhering to these practices, developers can harness the power of inheritance without compromising performance or maintainability.

Virtual Functions and Performance Considerations

Virtual functions in C++ enable dynamic polymorphism, allowing derived classes to override base class methods. However, their use introduces performance implications that must be carefully managed.

How Virtual Functions Work

Dynamic Dispatch: When a virtual function is called on a base class pointer or reference, the runtime determines the appropriate derived class function to execute.
Vtable (Virtual Table): The compiler generates a vtable for classes with virtual functions. Each object of such a

class includes a pointer to its class's vtable, used for function lookup during runtime.

Performance Overheads

Runtime Overhead:

Virtual function calls incur a small overhead due to the vtable lookup and function pointer dereferencing.
This is slower than a regular (non-virtual) function call, which is resolved at compile time.

Memory Overhead:

Each polymorphic class object contains an additional pointer (vptr) to its vtable, increasing memory usage.
The vtable itself occupies additional memory.

Inline Function Optimization:

Virtual functions cannot be inlined when called polymorphically, potentially impacting performance compared to non-virtual functions.

Cache Performance:

Virtual calls may disrupt CPU instruction caching due to indirect jumps, especially in tight loops.

Best Practices for Managing Performance

Use Virtual Functions Only When Necessary:

Avoid marking functions as virtual unless polymorphism is required.

Example:

cpp
Copy code
```cpp
class Base {
public:
    virtual void execute() = 0; // Only if dynamic behavior is required
};
```

Minimize the Use of Polymorphic Objects in

Performance-Critical Code:

Use static polymorphism (e.g., templates) for compile-time resolution when performance is critical.

Leverage final and override Keywords:

Mark virtual functions with final to prevent further overriding, enabling potential compiler optimizations.
Use override for clarity and to avoid accidental function hiding.

Example:

```cpp
Copy code
class Derived : public Base {
public:
    void execute() override final { /* Optimized implementation */ }
};
```

Avoid Excessive Inheritance Depth:

Reduce the complexity of inheritance hierarchies to simplify vtable management and improve runtime efficiency.

Profile and Optimize:

Use profiling tools to determine the impact of virtual functions on performance. Focus optimizations where necessary.

Alternatives to Virtual Functions

Static Polymorphism with Templates:

Achieve polymorphism without runtime overhead using compile-time techniques.

Example:

cpp
Copy code

```
template <typename T>
void execute(T& obj) {
   obj.run();
}
```

Function Pointers or Lambdas:

Use function pointers or lambdas for cases requiring limited dynamic behavior.

Conclusion

While virtual functions offer flexibility and extensibility, they come with inherent performance trade-offs. By carefully analyzing application requirements and adhering to best practices, developers can balance the benefits of virtual functions with the need for efficient and high-performance code.

CHAPTER 14

Profiling and optimizing C++ applications are essential steps to identify performance bottlenecks and improve efficiency. These processes involve analyzing the runtime behavior of an application and making targeted improvements.

Key Steps in Profiling

Choose a Profiling Tool: Use tools like Valgrind, gprof, Visual Studio Profiler, or Perf to analyze performance metrics.

Identify Hotspots: Profile the application to locate functions or code segments consuming excessive CPU or memory.

Analyze Call Stacks: Examine function call hierarchies to understand execution flow and dependencies.

Measure Resource Usage: Track memory allocation, CPU cycles, and disk I/O to detect inefficiencies.

Optimization Techniques

Algorithm Optimization:

Replace inefficient algorithms with more performant ones (e.g., $O(n)$ instead of $O(n^2)$).

Code Refactoring:
Eliminate redundant computations and improve readability.

Memory Management:

Use smart pointers and optimize dynamic memory allocations with efficient data structures.

Compiler Optimizations:

Enable compiler flags like -O2 or -O3 for better performance.

Parallelism:

Leverage multithreading or parallel algorithms to utilize CPU cores effectively.

Avoid Premature Optimization:
Focus on optimizing critical parts of the code identified during profiling.

Benefits

Improved execution speed.
Reduced resource consumption.
Enhanced scalability and maintainability.

Profiling tools combined with thoughtful optimization strategies lead to more robust and performant C++ applications.

Tools for Performance Profiling

Performance profiling tools help developers analyze and optimize the runtime behavior of C++ applications by identifying bottlenecks, inefficiencies, and resource-heavy operations.

Popular Performance Profiling Tools

Valgrind:

Features: Detects memory leaks, monitors memory usage, and analyzes performance.
Use Case: Ideal for identifying memory-related issues and optimizing resource usage.

Example:

bash
Copy code
valgrind --tool=callgrind ./your_program

gprof (GNU Profiler):

Features: Generates detailed reports of CPU time spent in functions and their call hierarchies.

Use Case: Best for profiling CPU-intensive applications.

Example:

bash
Copy code
```
g++ -pg program.cpp -o program
./program
gprof ./program gmon.out > report.txt
```

Perf (Linux Performance Tools):

Features: Tracks system-wide performance, including CPU, memory, and disk I/O.
Use Case: Ideal for low-level system profiling on Linux.

Example:

bash
Copy code

```
perf record ./your_program
perf report
```

Visual Studio Profiler:

Features: Integrated with the Visual Studio IDE, offering CPU, memory, and I/O profiling.
Use Case: Convenient for Windows-based C++ applications.

Example: Start profiling from the "Analyze" menu in Visual Studio.

Intel VTune Profiler:

Features: Advanced profiling for performance-critical applications, with insights into threading, memory, and GPU usage.
Use Case: Optimizing high-performance and multithreaded applications.

Instruments (macOS):

Features: Provides detailed profiling for macOS applications, including CPU, memory, and energy usage. Use Case: Profiling C++ applications developed for Apple platforms.

Clang's Sanitizers:

Features: Includes AddressSanitizer, ThreadSanitizer, and MemorySanitizer for detecting memory and thread-related issues.

Use Case: Debugging and optimizing memory safety.

Example:
bash
Copy code
clang++ -fsanitize=address program.cpp -o program
./program

Perfetto:

Features: A system profiling tool designed for tracing and analyzing performance across multiple processes.

Use Case: Comprehensive tracing of complex, multi-threaded systems.

Choosing the Right Tool

Memory Issues: Use Valgrind, Clang AddressSanitizer.
CPU Bottlenecks: gprof, Perf, or Intel VTune.
Multithreading: Intel VTune or ThreadSanitizer.
Platform-Specific: Visual Studio Profiler (Windows), Instruments (macOS).

Benefits of Profiling Tools

Increased Performance: Pinpoint and optimize costly operations.
Improved Resource Usage: Detect memory leaks and optimize allocations.
Better Scalability: Ensure efficient performance for larger workloads.

By selecting the appropriate tool for your needs, you can significantly improve the performance and reliability of your C++ applications.

Memory Optimization Techniques

Efficient memory usage is crucial for improving the performance and scalability of C++ applications. Memory optimization involves reducing unnecessary memory consumption, preventing leaks, and improving allocation efficiency.

Key Techniques

Use Smart Pointers:

Replace raw pointers with smart pointers (std::unique_ptr, std::shared_ptr, std::weak_ptr) to manage memory automatically and avoid leaks.

Example:

cpp

Copy code

```cpp
std::unique_ptr<int> ptr = std::make_unique<int>(10);
```

Avoid Unnecessary Dynamic Allocation:

Prefer stack allocation over heap allocation when possible, as stack allocation is faster and automatically managed.

Example:

cpp

Copy code

```cpp
int arr[100]; // Stack allocation
int* arr = new int[100]; // Heap allocation (avoid if unnecessary)
```

Optimize Data Structures:

Use appropriate containers like std::vector instead of raw arrays for better memory management and reduced overhead.

Shrink container capacity using shrink_to_fit when excess memory is no longer needed.

Memory Pooling:

Use memory pools to allocate and recycle memory blocks efficiently, reducing fragmentation and allocation overhead.

Avoid Memory Leaks:

Always match new with delete and use smart pointers to automatically free resources.

Tools like Valgrind or AddressSanitizer can help detect leaks.

Reduce Object Copies:

Pass large objects by reference instead of value to avoid unnecessary copying.

Use move semantics (std::move) to transfer ownership instead of copying data.

Example:

cpp
Copy code
void process(const MyClass& obj); // Pass by reference

Inline Small Functions:

Inline small functions to reduce the overhead of function calls and associated memory operations.

Efficient String Management:

Use std::string and reserve capacity upfront to avoid frequent reallocations.

Example:

cpp
Copy code

```
std::string str;
str.reserve(100); // Pre-allocate memory
```

Custom Allocators:

Use custom memory allocators for specialized scenarios where standard allocators are suboptimal.

Memory Alignment:

Align data structures to cache line boundaries to improve access speed and reduce cache misses.

Profile and Analyze:

Use tools like Valgrind, AddressSanitizer, or Intel VTune to profile memory usage and identify areas for improvement.

Best Practices

Minimize Global Variables: Avoid global/static variables that persist throughout the program's lifetime.

Use RAII (Resource Acquisition Is Initialization): Manage resources using RAII-compliant objects to ensure timely deallocation.

Benchmark and Test: Continuously test for performance impacts of memory optimization strategies.

By implementing these techniques, C++ developers can create applications that are both memory-efficient and high-performing, making them suitable for resource-constrained environments or large-scale systems.

Speeding Up Critical Code Paths

Critical code paths are sections of a program that significantly impact overall performance, often because they are executed frequently or handle intensive computations. Optimizing these paths can dramatically improve application efficiency.

Techniques to Speed Up Critical Code Paths

Profile First:

Use profiling tools (e.g., gprof, Valgrind, Perf) to identify the most time-consuming parts of the code.
Focus optimization efforts on these hotspots.

Optimize Algorithms and Data Structures:

Replace inefficient algorithms with faster ones (e.g., using hash maps instead of linear searches).
Choose data structures that minimize overhead and fit the use case.

Reduce Function Call Overhead:

Inline small, frequently called functions to reduce function call overhead.
Example:

cpp

Copy code

inline int square(int x) { return x * x; }

Minimize Memory Operations:

Reduce dynamic memory allocation in critical sections by using stack memory or memory pools.
Reuse objects instead of reallocating them frequently.

Leverage Move Semantics:

Use move constructors and move assignment operators to avoid expensive deep copies of objects.

Example:

cpp

Copy code

std::vector<int> v1 = std::move(v2);

Enable Compiler Optimizations:

Compile the code with optimization flags such as -O2 or -O3.

Example for GCC/Clang:

bash
Copy code
g++ -O3 program.cpp -o program

Use Multithreading or Parallelism:

Split tasks into threads or use parallel libraries (e.g., OpenMP, Intel TBB, or C++17 std::async) to utilize multiple CPU cores.

Example:

cpp
Copy code
#pragma omp parallel for
for (int i = 0; i < n; ++i) { process(i); }

Cache Optimization:

Access memory sequentially to improve cache performance and reduce cache misses.
Align data structures to fit cache lines.

Avoid Unnecessary Operations:

Minimize redundant computations by caching results of expensive calculations.

Use SIMD (Single Instruction Multiple Data):

Leverage SIMD instructions with libraries like Intel Intrinsics or compiler features for vectorized operations.

Precompute Values:

Calculate constant or predictable values at compile time or program initialization.

Profile Iteratively:

After implementing optimizations, re-profile the application to ensure improvements and identify new bottlenecks.

Example: Optimizing a Critical Code Path

Original Code:

cpp

Copy code

```cpp
for (int i = 0; i < arr.size(); ++i) {
    arr[i] = expensiveCalculation(i);
}
```

Optimized Code:

Replace expensiveCalculation with a precomputed lookup table.

Use parallelism for large datasets.

cpp

Copy code

```cpp
std::vector<int> lookupTable = precomputeValues();
#pragma omp parallel for
```

```
for (int i = 0; i < arr.size(); ++i) {
    arr[i] = lookupTable[i];
}
```

Benefits

Reduced execution time for performance-critical tasks.
Improved resource utilization.
Enhanced application scalability and responsiveness.
Focusing on these techniques ensures faster, more efficient C++ applications, especially in performance-sensitive domains like gaming, high-frequency trading, or scientific computing.